EUROPEAN COMMUNITY LAW

An Overview

European Community Law

An Overview

HLT PUBLICATIONS
200 Greyhound Road, London W14 9RY

First published 1989

ISBN 1 85352 532 4

British Library Cataloguing-in-Publication.

A CIP Catalogue record for this book is available from the British Library.

Printed and bound in Great Britain.

Contents

1 Introduction to Community Law

Background
Objectives
The legal nature of the Communities
Community law
Single European Act

Background

The condition of Europe in the aftermath of the Second World War warranted a radical re-assessment, by the combatant states, of their relationships with each other and more importantly of their relationship with the burgeoning power blocs to the East and West, the Soviet Union and the United States. Diverse initiatives were undertaken, whose overall objective was some type of integration of European States, which purported to serve the often mooted post-war ideal of a United Europe. These initiatives culminated in the signing, in 1957, by France, Italy, Germany, Belgium, Holland and Luxembourg of the Treaty of Rome. The European Economic Community came into existence at the beginning of 1958.

The Community was enlarged in 1973 by the accession of Denmark, Ireland and the United Kingdom to the Treaty of Rome. Norway did not ratify the Treaty after its electorate voted in a referendum not to do so. The current view is that since Norway's economic prospects are not so hopeful a renewed application will be made.

Greece was admitted in 1981, Spain and Portugal became members in 1986. As to future membership, article 237 provides that any European state may apply for membership and several European states have indicated a desire to become members. Chief among these are Austria and Turkey, although the latter's application is unlikely to be accepted in the forseeable future. The island states Malta and Cyprus are looking at the possibilities of membership; their accession would pose the most interesting problems of institutional representation on account of their relatively tiny populations.

Objectives

Article 2 of the Treaty of Rome sets out the task of the Community:

The Community shall have as its task, by establishing a common market and progressively approximating the economic policies of Member States, to promote throughout the Community:

a) a harmonious development of economic activities - see especially the Common Agricultural Policy and the Social Fund;

b) a continued and balanced expansion - this expansion is evidenced by the liberalisation of movement of people, goods, capital culminating in the creation of a single European market;

c) an increase in stability - see generally the measures attacking anti-competitive practices;

d) an accelerated raising of the standard of living; and

e) closer relations between the States belonging to it.

The activities to be undertaken to achieve the objects are set out in article 3 and include:

a) the elimination of:

customs duties: articles 12-17;
quantitative restrictions on imports and exports: articles 30-37;
measures having equivalent effect: articles 95-99;

b) establishment of a common customs tariff: articles 18-29;
establishment of a common commercial policy towards third world countries: articles 110-116;

c) the abolition, as between Member States, of obstacles to freedom of movement for persons: articles 48-51;
right of establishment: articles 52-58;
services: articles 59-66;
and capital: articles 67-73;

d) the adoption of a common policy in the sphere of agriculture: articles 38-47;

e) the adoption of a common policy in the sphere of transport: articles 74-84;

f) the institution of a system ensuring that competition in the common market is not distorted: articles 85-90: unfair competition; article 91: dumping; and articles 92-95: state aid;

g) the application of procedures by which the economic policies of Member States can be co-ordinated and disequilibria in their balances of payments remedied: article 102A economic and monetary policy. This amendment was introduced by the Single European Act 1986. Article 103 provides that Member States should consult on economic trends. Articles 104-109 concern the balance of payments;

h) approximation of laws of Member States to the extent required for the proper functioning of the common market: articles 100-102 (see especially the amendments to these articles made by the Single European Act 1986);

i) the creation of a European Social Fund in order to improve employment opportunities for workers and to contribute to the raising of their standard of living: articles 123-128;

j) the establishment of a European Investment Bank to facilitate the economic expansion of the Community by opening up fresh resources: articles 129, 130;

k) the association of the overseas countries and territories in order to increase trade and to promote jointly economic and social development: articles 131-136A.

Article 5 provides that the Member States will take all measures to facilitate the attainment of the Community's tasks.

Articles 2, 3 and 5 are important in the interpretation by the European Court of Justice of the rest of the Treaty, especially in actions brought against a Member State for failure to discharge its obligations to the Community.

The Community consisting of three Communities (European Coal and Steel Community, EEC and Euratom) is a type of international organisation which is committed to increasing economic and social integration. Considerable impetus has been given to this process by the passage of the Single European Act 1986 and its equivalent Acts in the other Member States. The Act provides for the creation of a single European market in goods and services. Political integration is a remote prospect, although the current President of the Commission Jacques Delors has stated that political integration is possible in the not too distant future. A keen student of European history and a realist, he was unwilling to suggest a date by which this unity may be achieved.

The legal nature of the Communities

The legal nature will be discussed from two viewpoints:

a) the relations between the Communities and the Member States, and

b) the relations of the Communities with non-member states.

The relations between the Communities and the Member States

The Communities are characterised, internally, by the setting up of permanent institutions which have been invested with legislative, executive and judicial powers. These powers have been transferred from the Member States in the areas which they have placed under Community competence. The transfer is, of necessity, based on the capacity of the Member States to set up international organisations, and its validity in international law depends on the formal ratification by the Member States of the Foundation Treaties. On ratification the transfer is definitive and irreversible. It is definitive as it is not subject to reservation by Member States or challenge in legal proceedings by the nationals of that State. It is irreversible because once the powers have been transferred, they cannot be renounced or lapse unless there are provisions in the Treaty to the contrary. The matters to which they relate cannot be returned to national competence.

Indeed although the European Coal and Steel Community Treaty has a life of fifty years, the European Economic Community Treaty and the Euratom Treaty have no such limitation; they have been concluded for an indefinite period. The Treaties have no mechanism for the withdrawal of a Member State. The EEC Treaty can be amended however: article 236.

Since the legal existence of the Communities is based on the transfer of sovereign powers, in certain areas two consequences must be noted:

i) The Communities can only exercise such powers as are expressly or by implication conferred on them by the Treaties. Their competence is only derived or 'attributed'. A wide interpretation may be placed on these competences where they are used in relation to an authority granted to achieve a Community objective. The Communities, however, cannot on their own authority assume any additional powers nor bring new areas within the ambit of their competence. The ambit may be widened by the Member States acting through their Representatives meeting in Council, a revision of the Treaty or by concluding new Treaties. Any action taken by the Community Institutions, which falls outside their competence, will lack legal foundation.

ii) Transfer of power to the Community has resulted in a corresponding limitation of the Member States' sovereign rights. A subsequent unilateral act incompatible with the Community cannot prevail. The Member State must by all available means facilitate the achievement of the Communities' tasks (see above). They must take all appropriate measures to ensure compliance with Treaty obligations and must, conversely, abstain from any measure which would jeopardise the attainment of Community objectives. This may entail being precluded from legislating in certain areas. These obligations are stated to be the natural corollary to the benefits derived from membership. In an area which is not within Community competence the Member State retains its legislative power.

The relations of the Communities with non-member states

The Communities appear as legal persons in their external relations. Their legal personality at the level of international law is derived from customary international law which ascribes such personality to international organisations and from the Foundation Treaties which expressly confer it on the Communities: article 6 ECSC Treaty and article 210 EEC Treaty which state simply that 'the Community shall have legal personality'; article 228 which provides that where the Treaty provides for the conclusion of an agreement with another State or international organisation the Commission shall negotiate and the Council will conclude that agreement. The Communities have the power and capacity to enter into international agreements. Such power is necessary to achieve the objectives of the Community, set out in Part 1 of the EEC Treaty, and is not confined to that expressly given but extends to what is necessary to achieve those objectives. In this case the power will arise by implication from provisions conferring internal powers and will include the power to co-operate with other countries.

While the Community's external Treaty-making power generally coincides with its internal law-making authority, the former may be exercised independently of the latter since it flows, by implication, from the Treaty provisions creating the internal power, Opinion 1/75 [1975] ECR 1355. This will mean that whenever the Community lays down common internal rules in implementation of a common policy envisaged by the Treaty, it acquires the power necessary to undertake external obligations towards non-member states, affecting those rules. The Community's Treaty-making power, once exercised, precludes any concurrent powers on the part of the Member States. To the extent that common internal rules come into being or a common policy is introduced, the Community alone will be in a position to assume and carry out contractual obligations towards non-member states affecting the whole sphere of application of the Community legal system. See generally *Commission* v *Council (European Road Transport Agreement)* Case 22/70 [1971] ECR 263 ('The ERTA Case') where it was held that, where the Community in pursuit of a common policy has concluded a treaty with a non-member state, a Member State may not enjoy a concurrent authority to do so.

Community law

Community law is a new, autonomous, supranational, uniform and unitary legal order with a limited field of application. Its provisions belong to neither public international law nor to municipal law. Community law and national law constitute two legal orders which are independent of each other. One is based on the Foundation Treaties; the other is based on a Constitution. It therefore follows from the independent nature of Community law that its system is based on the principle of a strict separation of the jurisdiction of the Communities' Institutions and that of the organs of the Member States. The Community Institutions, therefore, have no jurisdiction to interpret, apply, enforce, repeal or annul legislative or administrative acts of a Member State, nor to pronounce upon their validity under national law, even if such acts have been performed in the application of a Community provision. The Community Institutions can only require the Member States concerned, within the framework of Community proceedings, to adjust any national provisions that have been found contrary to Community Law. Conversely, while national organs have to interpret, apply and enforce Community law, they have in principle no jurisdiction to test the validity of Community provisions or their compatibility with national law, including constitutional law, and so cannot declare invalid or annul Community measures or suspend their application or enforcement. The validity of Community instruments can only be judged by the European Court and in the light of Community law. Any other course would undermine the legal basis of the Communities.

The supranational nature of Community law is emphasised by the fact that its subjects are not states, as in international law, nor individuals, as in municipal law, but Member States and their nationals. It defines the substantive powers, rights and obligations of its subjects and has created a system of sanctions, remedies and procedures enabling those subjects to enforce their rights, defend themselves against illegally imposed restrictions or obligations and deal with any infringement of the substantive rules.

Single European Act

a) The Single European Act is an expression of the political resolve voiced by the Member States notably at Fontainbleau in June 1984, in Brussels in March 1985, and at Milan in June 1985, to transform the whole complex of relations between their states into a European Union, in accordance with the Stuttgart Solemn Declaration of June 1983.

b) A distinction is drawn in the Single European Act between the status of political co-operation and matters relating to the European Community treaties.

c) The provisions amending the treaties establishing the European Communities can be divided into three categories. Firstly, those introducing into the treaties new policy objectives. Some of these already rank among Community policies in practice, but to incorporate them in the Treaty provides a firmer legal basis for their existence. Secondly, those affecting the decision-making of the Community and its legislative processes. Thirdly, other institutional matters.

d) The new policy objectives relate to the internal market, monetary capacity, social policy, economic and social cohesion, research and technological development (Titles I and II).

e) *The internal market*

Three additional articles of the Treaty (8A, 8B and 8C) lay down that 'The Community shall adopt measures with the aim of progressively establishing the internal market over a period expiring on 31st December 1992 ...'. The Commission is to report on progress before the end of 1988 and 1990. The Commission must also take into consideration 'the effort that certain economies showing differences in development will have to sustain ...' and may propose 'appropriate provisions'. However, if these are derogations, they must be of 'a temporary nature'. The 'measures' referred to above are subject to new decision-making procedures. In a declaration annexed to the Act, the signatory governments express their 'firm political will to take before 1st January 1993 the decisions necessary to complete the internal market ...': It should be noted that the articles concerning the completion of the Internal

Market are affected by a declaration annexed to the Act. This states that 'Nothing in these provisions shall affect the right of Member States to take such measures as they consider necessary for the purpose of controlling immigration from third world countries, and to combat terrorism, crime, the traffic in drugs and illicit trading in works of art and antiques.'

f) *Monetary capacity*

A new chapter is inserted into the Treaty (Chapter 1 in Part Three, Title II). This states that Member States co-operating to ensure the convergence of economic and monetary policies shall 'take account of the experience acquired in co-operation within the framework of the European Monetary System and in developing the ECU ...' (article 102A). Institutional change in this area, however, would be subject to the normal committee of governors of the central banks.

g) *Social policy*

An additional article (article 118A) states that 'Member States shall pay particular attention to encouraging improvements, especially in the working environment, as regards the health and safety of workers ...'. However, the final objective of harmonisation of working conditions will not prevent any state from maintaining or introducing higher standards. There is also a reference to the Commission's development of a dialogue between management and labour at the European level which could, if the two sides consider it desirable, lead to relations based on agreement (article 118B). The measures referred to in article 118A are subject to new decision-making procedures. These measures should also avoid creating burdens for small and medium-sized enterprises.

h) *Economic and social cohesion*

A new Title V (Economic and Social Cohesion) is added to Part Three of the EEC Treaty. This states that 'the Community shall develop and pursue its actions leading to the strengthening of its economic and social cohesion.' It shall also 'aim at reducing disparities between the various regions and the backwardness of the least-favoured regions' (article 130A). This is to be achieved by the policies of Member States and by the Community's structural funds. Once the Act enters into force, the Commission will carry out a review of the structural funds (the Agricultural, Social and Regional

Funds) in order to increase their efficiency and co-ordinate their operations. The Council will agree the results of this review by unanimity within one year.

i) *Research and technological development*

A new Title VI (Research and Technological Development) will be added to Part Three of the Treaty. In this the Community's objective is defined as being 'to strengthen the scientific and technological basis of European industry and to encourage it to become more competitive at international level' (article 130F). This will be achieved through carrying out research, technological development and demonstration programmes, the promotion of co-operation with third countries, the dissemination of the results of the research, etc, and stimulation of the training and mobility of researchers. The Community will adopt a 'multiannual framework programme'. This will lay down the scientific and technical objectives, define the priorities, set out the main lines of the activities envisaged and fix the amount of money deemed necessary. This programme may include provision for participation by third world countries or international organisations or by several Member States. The 'framework programme' will be adopted by unanimity.

j) *Environment*

A new Title VII (Environment) will be added to the Treaty. This lays down the objectives of Community action as follows: 'To preserve protecting human health; to ensure a prudent and rational utilization of natural resources.' This action will be based on the principles that preventive action should be taken, that damage should be rectified at source and that the polluter should pay. Environmental action should be carried out by the Community in cases where the objectives can be attained better than by individual Member States. There will be co-operation with third world countries and international organisations.

k) The agreement also states that the signatories 'consider that closer co-operation on questions of European security would contribute in an essential way to the development of a European identity in external policy matters. They are ready to co-ordinate their positions more closely on the political and economic aspects of security' (para 6a). The signatories are also 'determined to maintain the technological and industrial conditions necessary for their security' (para 6b).

l) The mechanism of political co-operation will be provided by meetings of political directors of foreign offices who will prepare the Ministers' discussions. In addition, 'a Secretariat based in Brussels shall assist the Presidency in preparing and implementing the activities of European Political Co-operation and in administrative matters' (para 10g).

m) The Single European Act, therefore, essentially codifies the existing practice of political co-operation with two exceptions: the specific mention of European security and the establishment of a secretariat.

The impact of the Single European Act on the institutions will be dealt with under the relevant headings in Chapter 2.

2 Institutions

Introduction

Article 4 of the Treaty states that the tasks entrusted to the Community will be carried out by the following institutions:

a) an Assembly;

b) a Council;

c) a Commission;

d) a Court of Justice.

The institutions are to act within the powers conferred on it by the Treaty.

The Assembly

Articles 137-144

a) *Composition*

The European Parliament (the Treaty refers to the Assembly but Parliament decided to adopt the title European Parliament in 1962) which sits in the Palais de Justice in Strasbourg, has 518 members. Prior to 1979 the members were appointed by the governments of the Member States. The numbers to be sent from each State were laid down by the Treaty, article 138, and were in vague proportion to the population of the Member State. The Council Decision and Act of 20 September 1976 on Direct Elections (76/787) provides in article 1 that the members of the Assembly should be elected by direct universal suffrage. Article 138(3) envisaged that the electoral system would through agreement become uniform throughout the Member States, ie some type of proportional representation with transferable votes. The United Kingdom's 'first past the post' system is of course at variance with the systems adopted by the other Member States. The difficulty in obtaining an agreement in this matter is reflected in the rather vague formulation of article 7(2) of 76/787: 'pending the entry into force of a uniform electoral procedure ... the electoral procedure shall be governed in each Member State by its national provisions.' Some slight convergence of views may be said to have been achieved, however, in that the European Assembly Elections Act 1978 provides that in Northern Ireland the single transferable vote system is to be used, s3.

The first direct elections took place in June 1979. Each Member of Parliament (MEP), referred to by the Treaty as representatives, is elected for a term of five years; article 3, 76/787. They have three main tasks: to advise the Council about the Commission's proposals for Community wide laws; to consider the Community budget, and to attempt to exert some control over the Council and Commission by means of questions about aspects of the Community's business.

b) *The role of Parliament: the supervisory function*

Article 137 states that the Assembly shall exercise the advisory and supervisory powers conferred on it by the Treaties. To give substance to these powers article 144 has given to the Assembly a powerful weapon in that they may by a two-thirds majority compel the Commission to resign as a body. This motion of censure is circumscribed by certain procedural requirements (article 144). There must be a three day period for reflection after the tabling of it and the two-thirds majority mentioned above must represent a majority of the members of the Assembly. Very few motions have been tabled, and none has been successful. The reasons for this are both practical and political. The practical reason would be that a breakdown of the political affiliations of the MEPs themselves would cover the political spectrum, left to right, and it would be almost impossible to forge a coalition of view to the extent required to pass an article 144 motion. The political reasons are rather more obtuse. Passing such a motion would involve a journey into the unknown because Commissioners are appointed by the governments of the Member States without reference to the Assembly. The governments may then appoint a new set of Commissioners whose policies and attitudes differ little from the outgoing Commissioners. Theoretically the Assembly could censure until a Commission was found which was acceptable to itself. A power struggle would develop between the Assembly and the national governments which could only end in a curtailment of the Parliament's limited powers. In practice the activities of the Community would be brought to a standstill.

The availability of the censure motion, however, has affected the manner in which the relationship of the Assembly and the Commission is perceived in that the Commission may be seen to be politically accountable to the Assembly. The advisory and supervisory powers set out in the following paragraphs and the development of parliamentary practice serve to confirm this.

c) *Annual general report*

Under the terms of article 18 of the Merger Treaty (the Treaty effective from 1 July 1967 whereby the institutions of the three original Communities were merged, this Treaty is part of the corpus of the Treaty establishing the EEC) the Commission must publish annually, not later than one month before the opening session of the Assembly, a general report on the activities of the Communities. The Assembly must discuss this report in open session; article 143. Since 1970, the Commission's President has also presented to Parliament an annual programme of the future activity of the Communities. The report is generally presented at the beginning of each year. This enables Parliament to scrutinise and comment on the framing of Community policies at an early stage and indeed challenge the proposals. The debate on the programme takes in the session in which it is presented, normally in February.

d) *Questions*

MEPs enjoy the right to be informed about the progress of the Commission's work. They may exercise this right by means of parliamentary questions. Article 140(3), Rules 45-47 of Parliament's rules of procedure, determines that the Commission must reply to questions put to it by the Assembly or its members. The questions must be replied to within a specified time. Questions may be for a written answer, oral answer with or without debate. The answers are published in the Official Journal. Written answers are the norm because the pressure on Parliament's time necessitates a limit to oral question time. The advantage of the oral question is that a related supplementary question may be asked. Questions may also be asked of the Council. A total of 4,599 questions were asked of both Institutions in 1985.

e) *The consultative function*

i) Parliament and legislation

The European Parliament has been traditionally asked to comment on proposals put forward by the Commission before the Council can make a decision on the final text. The Single European Act, which modifies the treaties, also provides for what is known as a co-operation procedure (see below). This procedure will ensure that the Council and Commission have to consider Parliament's amendments, subject inevitably to a unanimous vote by the Council. The areas where this procedure will mainly be used are, among others; freedom of establishment, questions concerning improvement of the working environment and regional policy. In future the agreement of Parliament will be needed for any international agreements and enlargement of the Community.

Excepting the co-operation procedure (above) and the assent procedure (whereby Parliament must approve new members and new association agreements) Parliament's influence on legislation is limited. Where a proposal has been submitted to Parliament, usually to a 'Parliamentary Committee' (see below), a report prepared by that committee will be debated by the full Parliament. Parliament's function in this area is however purely consultative. There is no power of decision, furthermore the opinions of Parliament may be disregarded by both Council and Commission.

Parliament does have a right to be consulted in certain legislative matters, see articles 43, 54, 56 and 87 of the Treaty. This right has been upheld in the so-called Isoglucose cases, especially *SA Roquette Freres* v *Council* [1980] ECR 3333, where the Court annulled a Council Regulation on the ground that an essential procedural requirement had been infringed. The Council had failed to consult the Assembly as required by article 43(2).

Further reference is made in the Treaty to Parliament's involvement in the process of legislation: article 155 of the Treaty provides that the Commission 'shall have its own power of decision and participate in the shaping of measures taken by the Council and by the Assembly in the manner provided for in the Treaty'. Article 149(2) lays down the procedure to be followed whenever Parliament is required to be consulted.

Notwithstanding the apparently minimal influence of the Parliament, the Council will, in practice, ask the Parliament's opinion even if not required to do so by the Treaties. Parliament, moreover, will sometimes address opinions to the Council of its own accord. The phraseology of the provisions in the Treaty concerning consultation - '... the Council shall on a proposal from the Commission and after consulting the Assembly ...' - gives the inference that it is the Council and not the Commission which is required to consult the Assembly. Consultation by the Commission, before submitting its proposals to the Council, is not excluded and article 149(3) - 'As long as the Commission has not acted, the Commission may alter its original proposal, in particular where the Assembly has been consulted on that proposal' - implies that the opinion of Parliament is important for the Commission which, keeping in mind its parliamentary accountability, may suggest that the views of the Assembly should be regarded seriously by the Commission.

The influence which Parliament can exert on the Council's decision-making may depend on the willingness of the Commission to support Parliament's views. The Council is not accountable to Parliament and Parliament cannot easily influence it, a circumstance which persists despite the fact that periodic reports are presented by the President of the Council and that Parliament may question the Council. Article 140 of the Treaty provides that 'the Council shall be heard by the Assembly in accordance with the conditions laid down by the Council in its Rules of Procedure'. Rule 19 of those Rules states that it can delegate the Council President or any other Member to be its representative at sessions of Parliament. There is therefore little formal arangement between the two Institutions (but see the conciliation procedure below), so in practice Parliament's influence will vary from case to case. It is the inconsistent nature of this influence that has caused Parliament to express its frustration at a lack of action by the Council on proposals for Community legislation on which Parliament has given a favourable opinion: eg in the field of harmonisation directives under article 100. This frustration was one of the factors which led Parliament to bring an action against the Council under articles 173 and 175 arising out of the Council's failure to adopt a common transport policy, article 75. In *European Parliament* v *Council* Case 13/83 [1985] 1 CMLR 138, the Court here held that, although the Parliament was one of the 'institutions' which could bring an action under article 175 and that the Council had failed in their duty to carry out the necessary measures within the required deadline, Parliament had itself failed to specify the necessary measures.

ii) *The budget*

Initially the European Community was financed by contributions from the exchequers of the Member States (see the scales for financial contributions laid down by article 200). It was always intended that these contributions should be replaced by the Community's own resources, article 201. 'Own resources' would include revenue from sugar market duties, common customs tariff duties etc. It was not until 1970 that a decision was taken to establish an 'own resource' system, now Council Decision on the Communities' system of own resources, 85.257 EEC Euratom. The 1970 decision was coupled with new rules under which the Parliament would acquire greater control over the budget. Parliament was not happy with these powers. The Commission took note and gave an undertaking that further proposals would be made within two years. Their failure to do so led to a motion of censure (supra) being tabled by Georges Spenale in December 1972. It was withdrawn when the President of the Commission, Sicco, said that the matter should properly be left to the enlarged Community to determine. A Financial Provisions Treaty of 1975 was agreed and came into force in 1977.

The Treaty gave Parliament increased powers over the budget and created the Court of Auditors. Parliament now has the final say on all 'non-compulsory' expenditure, ie administrative and operational expenditure - approximately 30 per cent of the budget. Regarding the rest of the budget Parliament can propose modifications which are then deemed to be accepted unless the Council rejects them by a qualified majority (see below). Finally Parliament can reject the Budget as a whole, article 203(8); 'the Assembly acting by a majority of its members and two-thirds of the votes cast, may, if there are important reasons, reject the draft budget and ask for a new draft to be submitted to it'.

Parliament took advantage of this power in December 1979 when it decided by 299 votes to 64 (1 abstention) to reject the Council's draft budget for 1980. Note must be taken however of the limit to Parliament's powers, see *Council* v *Parliament* Case 34/86 [1986] 3 CMLR 94 which indicated that strict budgetary procedure was to be observed by Parliament acting in concert with the Council.

Finally it is the Parliament's President who has the task of declaring that the budget has been adopted once all the procedures have been followed.

iii) *Budget timetable*

The making of the Community budget is a rather lengthy process stretching from early spring until late December. The budget goes through the following stages, generally ahead of schedule.

- By May, the Commission is required to calculate what is known as a 'maximum rate'. This governs the percentage by which 'non-compulsory' expenditure may be increased from one year to the next. 'Compulsory' expenditure, it should be noted, constitutes the greater part of the Community budget. (See p19.)
- By July, Parliament, the Council, the Court of Justice, the Court of Auditors, the Economic and Social Committee and the Commission are required to submit estimates of their expenditure for the year following. Except in the case of the Commission, these are simply administrative expenses and it is worth noting that Parliament is, subject to certain conditions, free to set its own budget. The Commission's estimates cover the whole range of Community policies, from agriculture to the search for oil, from regional aid to job creation schemes, from development aid to the fisheries policy - as well as its own administrative expenses.
- By September, the Commission consolidates the estimates in a preliminary draft budget. This will be the Commission's assessment of the cost of running the

Community's agreed policies and the Community's institutions.

- By 5 October, the Council is required to adopt a draft budget (if need be by a qualified majority of 45 votes out of 65) and forward it to Parliament.
- Within 45 days, Parliament will give the draft budget a first reading and it will usually call for changes to be made.
- Within 15 days, the Council will consider the changes Parliament is calling for.
- Within 15 days, Parliament will give the budget a second reading and make such final changes as it is empowered to make and as it thinks necessary. Parliament then either adopts or rejects the budget as a whole. If the budget is adopted by Parliament it is then executed by the Commission. If the budget is rejected, a new draft has to be submitted.

Parliament actually intervenes in the making of the budget from the beginning. It will table its own budget guidelines in March or April and will usually debate the Commission's consolidated estimates in July. It will then set on record its own opinion as to whether the expenditure envisaged is likely to be adequate to meet the policy objectives the Community has in view.

Parliament debates the Commission's preliminary estimates, setting its own appreciation on record before the estimates go to the Council to be turned into a draft budget. Once this draft has been formally presented to the House, the work of analysing it is split between Parliament's specialist committees (Committee on Agriculture for common agricultural policy spending, regional committee for the Regional Fund and so on). These committees will go into the draft budget in detail and report back to the Committee on Budgets so that a report, incorporating all committee views, can be presented to the House for the first reading. The Committee on Budgets, incidentally, appoints one of its members to pilot the budget through the House. He is known as the rapporteur. The first reading (usually in Parliament's October session) is the first real confrontation between Parliament and the Council, with Parliament tending (in every year so far) to side with the Commission over the money it is calling for to finance Community policies. The form has been for Parliament to conclude its first reading by asking the Council to reconsider its attitude and, in particular, to reinstate items proposed by the Commission but cut out by the Council. Parliament may also call for new expenditure in key areas like the search for oil.

After Parliament's first reading the draft budget goes back to the Council.

The Council considers Parliament's requests for changes: it has to muster a qualified majority of 45 votes out of 65 to reject amendments although the reverse is true of modifications, where the Council needs a qualified majority of 45 votes to accept them. Parliament, for its part, is required to muster a majority of its Members in support of amendments.

It is worth noting that there are two classes of expenditure in the community budget: compulsory and non-compulsory. The compulsory expenditure is that 'necessarily resulting from the Treaty of Rome or acts adopted in accordance therewith' and includes such items as the common agricultural policy. The non-compulsory is expenditure other than that 'necessarily resulting from the Treaty'; this includes such items as the Regional Fund, social policy, research and development aid.

Parliament has the power to request changes (in the form of modifications) in compulsory expenditure and to make changes (in the form of amendments) in non-compulsory expenditure. Any increase in expenditure by virtue of such changes will be subject to a ceiling (calculated in relation to the maximum rate referred to earlier). The calculation is a complex one, its purpose being to contain any increase in non-compulsory expenditure within reasonable bounds.

A new 'maximum rate' can be agreed between the Council and Parliament - and has been agreed every year since the rules came into operation.

Second reading

For Parliament, the crucial stage in the making of the budget is the second reading. At this stage the Council will have considered Parliament's requests for changes in its draft budget and - if the practice of recent years is anything to go by - it may well have resisted any bid to raise the overall total figure.

Parliament then reconsiders the draft budget as a whole and may reinstate such amendments as it considers indispensable to the success of the Community's policies. Where these involve increases above the 'maximum rate', a new rate is agreed with the Council - usually in special consultations during Parliament's December session.

An outline of the stages the budget goes through would be incomplete without a reference to the meetings held by the Committee on Budgets prior to the first and second readings. It is at these meetings, where the Council and the Commission are represented, that the committee's overall view of the budget takes shape. This is worth drawing attention to because Parliament has usually taken account of the views of its Committee on Budgets in coming to its final judgment on the budget as a whole. Parliament's decision to reject the draft budget for 1980 was a case in point.

As important as sharing in making the budget or amending it is the job of keeping an eye on the Commission to see that the budget Parliament adopts is actually put into effect.

For control over actual expenditure is another of the powers vested in the European Parliament under the Treaty of July 1975. To check that budget money is spent as agreed, Parliament has created a Committee on Budgetary Control. This committee advises whether a 'discharge' may be given to the various institutions of the Community with respect to their budgets. In the case of the Commission, a refusal by Parliament to give a discharge might well be regarded as tantamount to a censure motion.

Parliament is assisted in exercising its powers of control over the implementation of the budget by the Court of Auditors. The members of the Court of Auditors are appointed by the Council after consulting Parliament.

Budgetary co-operation

Another important aspect of Parliament's powers concerns co-operation with the Council in regard to the budget. On 22

April 1970 the Council adopted a resolution to the effect that 'in matters of budgetary procedure everything possible should be done by common agreement between the Council and the European Parliament to ensure close co-operation at all levels between the two institutions; in particular the President or another member of the Council should be present at the deliberations of the European Parliament on the draft budget.'

Further to this resolution the practice has been for a delegation of MEPs to meet regularly with members of the Council in the autumn of every year when the budget is being worked out. These meetings take on a special importance when the budget is in its closing stages. This procedure needs to be distinguished, however, from the 'conciliation procedure' covering relations between the institutions in the discussion of 'acts having substantial financial implications' (see below for an account of the 'conciliation procedure').

iv) *Conciliation procedure*

On 4 March 1975 a Joint Declaration was made by the European Parliament, the Council and the Commission establishing a conciliation procedure between the Parliament and the Council which sets out increased budgetary powers for Parliament, and generally provides for closer working practices between Parliament and Council in important decisions relating to expenditure. The instrument of conciliation is the Conciliation Committee which consists of the Council and representatives of the European Parliament. The aim of the procedure is to seek agreement between the Parliament and the Council (article 6).

To date, the conciliation procedure has been applied in four cases, namely in respect of the amendments to the 1973 Financial Regulation during the latter part of 1977, at the time of the setting up, in 1974/1975, of the Regional Development Fund, but more particularly in connection with its recent modification, in respect of a new loan instrument to finance Community investments and in relation to the proposals to grant financial and technical aid to non-associated developing countries. In more than twenty further cases the Commission has drawn the attention of the other two institutions to the fact that, because criteria set out in paragraph 2 of the Declaration were met in a specific proposal, the procedure could, where appropriate, be instituted. In many of these cases the Parliament has not, of its own volition (no mention having been made in its opinion), insisted on the holding of the procedure.

v) *Committees*

According to Rule 37(1) of the Rules of Procedure, Parliament may set up standing or temporary, general or special committees and define their powers and duties. There are 18 standing committees including inter alia the following: Political Affairs, Legal Affairs, Budgets, Environment, Women, Institutional Reform. From time to time Parliament will set up a temporary committee to deal with matters that fall outside the ambit of the permanent committees.

The reports of the committees will serve as the basis for the majority of the debates in Parliament. Any member may table a motion for a resolution on a matter falling within the range of Community activities. That motion will then be referred to the appropriate committee. A similar procedure is followed when the Council asks for an opinion on a matter. A report will then be prepared. Each committee will appoint one of its members to be responsible for a particular report. That person is known as the rapporteur and he/she will lead the debate when the matter comes before Parliament.

The Council

Articles 145-154 (articles 2-6 Merger Treaty)

a) *Composition*

The members of the Council are delegates of their States. They will act on the instructions of their Governments. Unlike the Commission the members will vary from time to time. It will depend on the nature of the meeting. If the meeting is to discuss general matters then the Foreign Ministers of the Member States will be likely to attend but if the meeting is to consider a specialist matter, for example agricultural policy, then it will be attended by the appropriate minister of the Member State.

b) *Functions of the Council*

The functions are set out in article 145 namely:

'to ensure co-ordination of the general economic policies of the Member States and have power to take decisions.'

It is the exercise of this latter power that tells us the major function of the Council, which is as legislator of the Community.

This function is underlined by the fact that it is the Council which will produce regulations and directives which are the result of close liaison with the Committee of Permanent Representatives (COREPER). The function of this latter body is to assist the Council in the preparation of its work and to facilitate communication between the Institutions of the Community and the Governments of the Member States.

c) *Conduct of meetings*

Each Member State will hold the office of President of the Council for a term of six months. The presidency of the Council rotates among the Member States. The holding of the presidency means assuming the burden of co-ordinating and presiding over the meetings. These meetings can take place anywhere within the Community but will usually take place in Brussels.

Article 148(1) states:

'save as otherwise provided by this treaty the Council shall act by a majority of its members.'

It will rarely act by a simple majority. Unanimity used to be the rule until it was found Community business was hopelessly slow. The Council began to act more frequently by means of a qualified majority defined by article 148(2) of the Treaty. To understand the nature of the qualified majority it is necessary to understand the weighting of the votes.

The votes are weighted in the following manner:

Germany, France, Italy, UK	-	10	votes each
Spain	-	8	votes
Belgium, Greece, the Netherlands, Portugal	-	5	votes each
Denmark, Ireland	-	3	votes each
Luxemburg	-	2	votes
Total	-	76	votes

In order to achieve a qualified majority 54 votes are needed, thereby ensuring that the larger States cannot coerce the smaller members.

The Single European Act which amended the Treaty provides that majority voting will be extended to certain matters, in particular those matters relating to the internal market.

Unanimity is usually required in matters of great importance, for example, the admission of a new Member State to the Community, concluding a treaty with a third state or international organisation (article 238) and matters concerning the approximation of laws (article 100).

The inter-relationship of the Commission and Council is marked by article 149 which states:

'where in pursuance of this treaty the Council acts on a proposal of the Commission unanimity shall be required for an act constituting an amendment to that proposal.'

d) *Luxembourg Accords*

If the vital interest of a Member State is threatened, a convention exists within the Community whereby a Member State may effectively veto a measure to which it objects. This convention is known as the Luxembourg Accords, which, in fine, provides that where very important interests are at stake discussion should be continued until a unanimous decision is reached.

Articles 228, 235

Article 228 provides that agreements between the Community and other states or international organisations will be negotiated by the Commission but concluded by the Council. Consultation will be made with the Assembly, if the Treaty so provides.

Article 235 indicates the wide powers of the Council because under this article it can, if necessary, take appropriate measures to achieve the objects of the Community, even though the Treaty does not provide the necessary powers. It will act unanimously on a proposal from the Commission after consultation with the Assembly: see *Hauptzollamt Bremerhaven* v *Massey-Ferguson* Case 8/73 [1973] ECR 879.

In practice article 235 is viewed restrictively by the Council. It is assumed not to apply when the introduction of new obligations going beyond those defined in the Treaty is considered. The Court considered the article in the above case and concluded that the article cannot be used if there is already a power in an existing Treaty provision.

The Commission

Articles 155 (articles 9-18 Merger Treaty)

a) *Composition*

The Commission consists of at least one citizen from each Member State. Presently there are 17 members: two from Britain, France, Germany, Italy and Spain and one from Belgium, Denmark, Greece, Ireland, Luxemburg, Netherlands and Portugal.

b) *Appointment*

Each member of the Commission is appointed by agreement between the Governments of the Member States. The term of office is four years, renewable, during which time the Commissioners may only be removed en masse by a vote of the European Parliament. Such an expression of no confidence requires a two thirds majority of the Parliament, supra, article 144. The individual Commissioners cannot be removed by their own national governments and herein may be seen the effect of article 10(2) which ensures that the Commissioners are independent in the performance of their functions and will not 'seek nor take instructions from any Government or from any other body'. They must not take any action incompatible with their duties. It is not unusual for Governments to make attempts to ensure that 'their Commissioner' follows a particular line. Consider the UK Government's recent behaviour concerning the non re-appointment of its two Commissioners. Commissioners in practice have been notoriously independent. It remains to be seen whether this circumstance will remain. An individual Commissioner may be compelled to retire by the European Court if he/she infringes article 10(2) or is generally incompetent.

A President may be appointed from among their number by the mutual agreement of the Member States for two years, renewable.

c) *Functions*

These are defined by article 155.

In order to ensure the proper functioning and development of the common market, the Commission shall:

i) ensure that the provisions of this Treaty and the measures taken by the institutions pursuant thereto are applied;

ii) formulate recommendations or deliver opinions on matters dealt with in this Treaty, if it expressly so provides or if the Commission considers it necessary;

iii) have its own power of decision and participate in the shaping of measures taken by the Council and by the Assembly in the manner provided for in this Treaty;

iv) exercise the powers conferred on it by the Council for the implementation of the rules laid by the latter.

Briefly, the function of the Commission is to ensure that the rules and principles of the Community are respected and that the rules are applied correctly. If a Member State wants a waiver or derogation from the rules then the Commission will decide the matter.

The Commission is the 'watchdog of the Treaties' and as such has powers of detection; see articles 4, 14(6), 15(1), 31, 72, 73(2), 93(3), 109(2), 111(50) and 115 where a duty to keep the Commission informed concerning certain matters is imposed on Member States.

The Commission also enjoys powers of investigation. Article 213 empowers the Commission to gather information and carry out checks which are necessary for the performance of the tasks entrusted to it, subject, of course to the provisions of the Treaty. Sometimes Member States or individuals will bring matters to the attention of the Commission by way of complaint or Parliament will submit a written question (article 140). The Commission, after investigation, can impose fines on individuals and companies against which an appeal may be made to the European Court of Justice. The Commission has powers under article 169 to ensure that the Member States comply with their obligations.

There are three distinct stages to the article 169 procedure.

i) *The informal stage*

This stage is the conciliation stage where the Commission will write to the Member State giving that State an opportunity to comment on its violation.

ii) *The reasoned opinion stage*

The Commission will issue a reasoned opinion. This document will indicate that the Member State is in violation of its Treaty obligations and the document will further state wherein the violation occurs. The Commission will give a time limit within which the State must respond. At this stage most Member States will remedy the violation.

iii) *The Court of Justice*

If the State fails to comply in time the Commission now has the option to bring the matter to the ECJ. There is no obligation to do so as the Commission can exercise a discretion taking into account the relative importance of the matter and the necessity to discourage other States from similar violations.

Article 171 directs that if the Court finds against the State then the State must obey the judgment of the Court.

See:

The Commission v *France* [1975], *The Merchant Sailor Case* Case 167/73 [1974] ECR 359

The Commission v *Italy* [1968], *The Art Treasures Case* Case 7/68 [1968] ECR 423

Van Gend en Loos [1963] Case 26/62 [1963] CMLR 105

The Commission v *United Kingdom*, *The Tachograph Case* Case 128/78 [1979] 2 CMLR 45

The Commission's role as decision-maker and participant in the shaping of measures taken by the Council and the Assembly is to be found in its power under article 189 to make, together with the Council, regulations, issue directives, take decisions or deliver opinions, and in the widening of its law-making role under the Single European Act. The Commission is often referred to as the initiator of Community law which is made in the following manner:

i) A proposal will be presented to the Commission who will consider it and if the matter is to be taken further it will be forwarded to ...

ii) The Council who will then take note and refer the matter to ...

iii) The Parliament who debate the matter and will vote and will pass an opinion back to ...

iv) The Council. The opinion of Parliament is not binding on either the Commission or the Council. The matter to be legislated will usually be referred to committees such as the Economic and Social Committee and any relevant organisations. The matter will then be referred to ...

v) The Committee of Permanent Representatives (COREPER). These are Member State Government nominees who will act on the instructions of the governments appointing them. This Committee will settle as many matters pertinent to the proposed legislation as they can. Those matters which have not been settled will be settled (or at least an attempt will be made to settle) at a subsequent meeting of the Council where the final decision will lie, article 149.

This procedure is the traditional procedure, but following the Single European Act there is a co-operation procedure which applies to legislation in several important areas of community activity, particularly those relating to the single market. This procedure is (briefly) as follows.

1 The Commission will formulate a proposal which will then be passed to Parliament ...

2 who will pass an opinion back to the Commission who will ...

3 pass it on to the Council who will adopt a common position by a qualified majority. The matter will then be referred back to ...

4 Parliament within three months who ...

- will approve Council's position; Council will then adopt the Act, or ...
- will reject Council's position in which case Council must act unanimously, or ...
- will amend Council's common position by an absolute majority of its members in which case the matter will be referred ...

5 back to the Commission within one month who will review Parliament's amendments and may as a result revise its proposal in which case the matter will be referred back to the Council within three months who may ...

- adopt the Commission proposal by a qualified majority, or ...

- adopt Parliament's amendments which have not been approved by the Commission unanimously, or ...
- amend the Commission proposal unanimously, or ...
- fail to act.

6 If the Council fails to act, the Commission's proposal lapses.

Article 155(4) describes an executive function which can be divided into two parts:

i) the Commission has powers conferred by the Treaties directly, the chief of which concern the customs union and competition; and

ii) powers conferred by the Council for the execution of the acts of the Council. This power to delegate is significant as generally it is the Council who must ensure that the objectives of the Treaties are attained and to this end must take decisions; see article 145 as amended by the Single European Act. In practice the Council does not have the means of executing the details of its decisions and does not set up machinery for their implementation; the Commission usually undertakes these tasks. It is important to note that any delegation of powers by the Council to the Commission is subject to the principle that those powers in turn cannot be sub-delegated, eg to a Member State, *Rey Soda* v *Cassa Conguaglio Zucchero* Case 23/75 [1975] ECR 1279.

d) *Procedure*

Decisions are made by a simple majority although frequently a written procedure will be employed in which draft decisions will be circulated and, if no objection is registered, the decision will be adopted.

To assist its work the Commission has an administrative staff of about 11,000 officials divided among 20 Directorates General. They still claim that they have not enough staff!

The European Court of Justice

Articles 164-188

a) *Composition*

The European Court of Justice, which sits in Luxembourg, has 13 judges who are assisted by six advocates-general. They are appointed for six years by the Member States. Like the Commission their independence is assured.

It is the duty of the advocates-general, 'acting with complete impartiality and independence, to make, in open court, reasoned submissions on cases brought before the Court of Justice'. Their activities are of great importance especially because their impartial submissions as regards facts, as well as legal argument, can form a valuable basis for the decision to be taken by the Court in the first and last instance.

The appointment of the judges and the advocates-general is by mutual agreement (article 166 EEC) among the governments of the Member States, for a period of six years. They are chosen from 'persons whose independence is beyond doubt and who possess the qualifications required for appointment to the highest judicial offices in their respective countries or who are jurisconsults of recognised competence' (article 167 EEC). Provisions relating to the taking of the oath, privileges and immunities, incompatible secondary functions, and deprivation of office are intended to ensure the independence of both judges and advocates-general. On the other hand the relatively short term of office which has been provided for is of doubtful wisdom, as is the fact that the appointment of judges and advocates-general has been placed entirely in the hands of the governments. In this way, too small an institutional guarantee of their independence is given. Very great confidence indeed is thus placed in the disinterestedness of the governments with respect to their appointment and in the moral qualities of the persons appointed, a confidence which fortunately has so far been justified.

Council decision of 24 October 1988 establishes a court of first instance. Decision of 7 November 1989 determines that the court will sit as two chambers of five judges and three chambers of three judges.

b) *Duties and powers*

The Court ensures the observance of law in the interpretation and application of the Treaties and their implementing rules (articles 31 ECSC, 164 EEC and 136 EAEC). To this end, a number of powers have been conferred on the Court. These are mainly intended to enable the Court to judge the acts and omissions of the institutions and the Member States in accordance with Community law and to ensure uniformity of interpretation of Community law in the application of this law by municipal courts. The conditions under and the manner in which the Court is required to exercise the powers, which form part of this hard core of its jurisdiction, will be discussed later. In the present context a broad survey of the various powers of the Court will be given and a number of aspects of its jurisdiction and of the functions it performs within the Communities will be dealt with. Attention will be devoted mainly to the provisions of the EEC Treaty. (It should be borne in mind that proposals for creating a court of first instance exist and are awaiting final agreement.)

The powers of the Court can be divided into three categories: the settling of disputes, the giving of binding opinions (exceptionally), and the giving of preliminary rulings. It appears that the jurisdiction of the Court extends to disputes that may arise as to the interpretation and application of Community law between institutions, between Member States, and between institutions on the one hand and Member States and private parties on the other. It is characteristic of the Court of Justice of the European Communities that it is relatively accessible to private persons who wish their Community rights to be upheld. In this it differs from most international courts, before which (apart from the case of administrative tribunals settling disputes between international organisations and their officials) private persons cannot as a rule appear as parties to the proceedings.

In the domain of settling disputes the Court acts in the first place as the administrative court (in the continental sense) for the Communities, whose duty is to protect the legal subjects, Member States as well as private persons, against the illegal acts or omissions of the institutions. Such an administrative jurisdiction is exercised as a rule by the Court if it takes cognizance of:

i) an appeal for a declaration that, in violation of the Treaty, the Council or the Commission has failed to act (article 175

EEC); appeal against inaction;

ii) an appeal for annulment of the legal acts of the Council and the Commission (article 173 EEC);

iii) an appeal against administrative penalties, an instance of 'unlimited' jurisdiction (article 172 EEC);

iv) a claim for damages on the strength of the non-contractual liability of the Communities (article 178 EEC);

v) an action based on an arbitration clause in a contract concluded by or on behalf of the Communities (article 181 EEC);

vi) disputes between the Communities and their officials (and any other servants) (articles 179 and 215 paragraph 3 EEC).

The Court is to be compared to an international court if the following cases are brought before it:

vii) disputes between Member States in connection with the subject matter of the Treaties, which are submitted to the Court under a special agreement (article 182 EEC);

viii) disputes between the Commission and Member States or between Member States themselves about a Member State's failure to fulfil its obligations under the Treaty (articles 169-170 EEC).

The Court acts as a constitutional court if it has to deliver an opinion on the question:

ix) whether agreements concluded by the EEC are compatible with the Treaty (article 228, paragraph 2, EEC).

The function of the Court as a constitutional court is not, however, exhausted by these heads of jurisdiction. In contentious proceedings, chiefly in an appeal for annulment or in an action to have a violation of a Treaty by a Member State placed on record (see 8 infra), the Court helps to safeguard the maintenance of the basic structural provisions of the three Treaties as well as the complicated balance of powers between the institutions inter se and between the Communities and the Member States as laid down therein.

Further, an appeal for annulment in certain cases creates a particular opportunity to check whether the 'community legislation' is in agreement with the Treaties. Such checking concerns the 'constitutionality' of quasi-legislative acts which originate with a public authority and which have a normative effect, erga omnes, as the Court has stated. It is on this very ground that an appeal for annulment of such acts has been virtually refused to private persons under the Treaties. Although, looked at from the point of view of their form, the activities of the Court in the contentious proceedings here mentioned more or less resemble those of an administrative or international court, looked at from the viewpoint of their context, in the cases here discussed they show a resemblance to a 'constitutional' jurisdiction.

The Court only possesses those powers which have been explicitly conferred on it or in virtue of specific Treaty provisions ('competences d'attribution'). In the majority of the cases discussed above the jurisdiction of the Court is based directly on the European Treaties. It is then possible to speak of obligatory or private jurisdiction, ie a jurisdiction which is exercised by the Court to the exclusion of national (article 183 EEC) or international (article 219 EEC) judicial bodies. In a number of cases, however, the Treaties also provide for an optional jurisdiction of the Court, ie a jurisdiction the compulsory character of which depends on the existence of a particular unilateral or multilateral juridicial act other than a Treaty provision, which then forms the jurisdictional title.

The jurisdiction of the Court so far discussed does not embrace all cases in which there may be a question of judicial application to community law. In disputes between Member States and private persons or between private persons themselves questions in relation to the interpretation and application of Community law may arise before a municipal court. In this field, too, a specific type of jurisdiction has been conferred on the Court. It is competent:

x) to pronounce by way of a preliminary ruling on the interpretation of the Treaty provisions and on the validity and the interpretation of the acts of the institutions of the Communities if a question on this subject is raised before a municipal judicial body (article 177 EEC).

Such a body can or (if it functions as a jurisdiction from which there is no recourse which need not be a court of final instance) must address the Court. Thanks to this jurisdiction the Court can be enabled to promote the uniformity of interpretation of Community law in the legal practice of the Member States. In connection with the discussion of the preliminary ruling we shall see that as a consequence of this jurisdiction the Court can moreover, in co-operation with the national courts, make a real contribution to the judicial control of the observance of Community law by the Member States, and thus to the legal protection of individuals against acts of those Member States which conflict with Community law.

c) *Jurisdiction and procedure*

The task of the Court of Justice is, in general, to ensure that, in the interpretation and application of the Community Treaties and of the rules laid down for their implementation, the law is observed. This implies that the Court has as its duty, on the one hand, to control the legality of the conduct of the institutions as well as the conformity with Community law of that of the Member States and, on the other hand, to safeguard the rights and legitimate interests of all those subject to Community jurisdiction (ie the Communities themselves, the Member States, and private individuals).

In order to enable the Court of Justice to carry out its tasks, the Treaties have conferred upon it a precisely delimited jurisdiction. The exercise of that jurisdiction is governed by the simultaneous operation of three fundamental principles which pervade all its aspects and basically determine the nature and scope of the various forms of actions. These principles are:

i) *Separation of powers*

This has two aspects. Firstly, in relation to the national courts there is a restriction on the jurisdiction of both courts. The European Court has no jurisdiction to interpret, apply, enforce, repeal or annul legislative or administrative acts of the Member States nor to pronounce upon their validity under national law. These functions are confined to the national courts' jurisdiction.

Secondly, in the relationship between the Community institutions separation of power gives effect to the fundamental principle of institutional balance which governs all aspects of Community activity. Thus in actions concerning the legality of the institutions' conduct (actions for annulment and for failure to act) the jurisdiction of the Court of Justice is strictly limited.

ii) *Exclusiveness of powers*

It follows from the principle of the separation of powers that in all those cases where the European Court has been given jurisdiction by or under the Treaties its jurisdiction is exclusive.

iii) *Express conferment of powers*

The Court, just as the other institutions of the Communities, may act only within the limits of the powers conferred upon it by the Treaties. This has as a consequence the limitation of the Court's jurisdiction to expressly conferred situations or where there is a particular provision of the Treaties. There is, therefore, no 'residual' or 'reserve' power - no competence to entertain cases not expressly coming under its jurisdiction in order to afford judicial protection to private individuals who might otherwise be deprived of all legal redress at both national and Community level.

The jurisdiction of the Court of Justice encompasses a variety of proceedings which may usefully be grouped into three broad classes according to formal procedural criteria. These are:

- direct actions
- references for preliminary rulings; and
- requests for advisory opinions.

These are considered in subsequent chapters.

d) *Admissibility of action*

It follows from the above that the Court of Justice has jurisdiction to entertain any given action only insofar as the applicant has been granted by the Treaties the right to bring that particular action and the various conditions laid down have been complied with. This requires the court to examine whether it has jurisdiction before considering the substantive issues; in other words whether the action is admissible. As will be seen, in relation to specific remedies, a decision as to the admissibility of an action is made primarily with reference to the person of the applicant and the practice and subject matter of his claim and not with reference to the submissions and arguments that he puts forward in support of that claim.

e) *Representation*

Representation before the Court of Justice is compulsory at all stages of the proceedings, whether written or oral, and for all parties. The Member States and the institutions of the Communities are represented by an agent appointed for each case, who may, advised by a lawyer, be entitled to practise before a court of a Member State.

The professional status (eg admission to, suspension or disbarment from, practice) of a lawyer is determined according to his own national law.

f) *Written procedure (rules of procedure of the Court of Justice OJ 1974 350/1)*

The ordinary procedure before the Court of Justice consists of two main parts: written and oral. Where necessary, preparatory inquiries may take place between the two parts.

Generally speaking, the written stage, which is not open to the public, is by far the most important part of the procedure before the Court of Justice. It consists of the communication by the Registrar to the parties, and to the institutions whose measures are in dispute, of the various pleadings, such as applications, defences, statement of case, as well as of all papers and documents submitted therewith.

Within a month of service by the Registrar of the application on the defendant, a defence must be lodged; failure to do so may lead to the Court giving judgment in default.

The written procedure ends with the Judge Rapporteur's preliminary report as to whether a preliminary inquiry is necessary. When the Court orders such an inquiry, the Court may undertake it itself, or may assign it to a Chamber which may then exercise the powers vested in the Court. Where the Court decides to open the oral procedure without an inquiry, the President of the Court is required to fix the opening date.

g) *Preparatory inquiries*

The purpose of these inquiries is to determine issues of fact where the Court finds this necessary in order to enable it to give judgment. The measures that may be adopted include the personal appearance of the parties, request for information and production of documents, and experts' reports.

h) *Oral procedure*

The oral procedure consists of the reading of the reports presented by the Judge Rapporteur and the hearing by the Court of agents, advisers and lawyers and of the opinion of the Advocate-General, as well as the hearing, if any, of witnesses and experts. On the whole, the hearing is normally brief as the main arguments of the parties are already set out in the written pleadings.

Upon the conclusion of the oral procedure the Court proceeds to the deliberation of the case. These deliberations are secret. The opinion reached by the majority of the judges after final discussion determines the decision of the court. A single judgment is always given and no separate or dissenting opinions are published.

The judgment consists of three main parts:

i) a summary of the facts and of the conclusions, submissions and arguments of the parties;

ii) the grounds for the decision; and

iii) the operative part including the decision as to costs.

i) *Costs*

In all contentious proceedings before it, the Court of Justice must adjudicate upon costs even if the parties have made no submissions in this respect. As a matter of practice the judgment or order of the Court merely states who is to bear the costs, without quantifying them. Generally speaking, there are three main rules as to how costs are to be disposed of between the parties:

i) The unsuccessful party is ordered to pay the costs, but only if they have been asked for in the successful party's conclusions. Where a successful party has made no formal submissions on this matter, he must bear his own costs. Where neither party has made any submission on costs, each must be ordered to bear his own costs.

ii) Where each party succeeds on some or fails on other heads, the Court may apportion the costs.

iii) The Court may order even a successful party to pay costs which the Court considers that party to have unreasonably or vexatiously caused the opposite party to incur.

j) *Interim measures*

Under article 186 of the Treaty the Court of Justice may in any cases before it prescribe any necessary interim measures. An application for such a measure may only be made by a party in a case before the court. Such measures will only be granted if a prima facie case is made out for such a measure and the measure is necessary to avoid serious and irreparable damage, see case 293/85 R *Commission* v *Belgium* [1985] ECR 3521.

3 The United Kingdom and Community Law

Introduction
The European Communities Act 1972

Introduction

In the case of *McWhirter* v *Attorney-General* (1972) it was made clear by Lord Denning that although the Treaty of Rome had been signed it would have no effect, as far as the courts were concerned, until it had been made an Act of Parliament. However, once it had been implemented by an Act, the courts would go by that Act. This formulation supports the contention that Community law enters the municipal legal systems of the member states by incorporation of the foundation treaties by an Act of Parliament.

In the UK the conclusion and ratification of an international treaty is generally within the prerogative of the Crown, so a constitutional doctrine has had to be evolved whereby a treaty will only form part of English law if an enabling Act of Parliament is passed. The rule that obligations do not directly affect the subjects of the Crown derives from historical circumstances and has no ideological foundations. Its aim was to prevent the Crown from legislating without the consent of Parliament and the rule is generally applicable to all international treaties which affect private rights or liabilities or have as their effect a charge on public funds or need some modification of the common law or statute for their enforcement in the courts.

This dualist approach to conventional international legal obligations is augmented by the doctrine of 'incorporation' or 'adoption' in regard to customary rules of international law. Such customary rules are considered to be part of the law of the land, and are enforced as such only in so far as it is not inconsistent with Acts of Parliament or prior judicial decisions of final authority. However, the formal incorporation of a treaty by Act of Parliament does not of itself establish a hierarchical order as between treaty law and national law. This is because in strict constitutional theory under certain conditions a statute may bind the courts even if it is in conflict with subsequent treaty law. In addition treaty law may have to give way in the event of conflict to decided precedents. Contrast this dualist approach to the monist approach adopted by the Belgian courts in the case of *Minister for Economic*

Affairs v *Fromagerie Franco-Suisse* (1972) and the related action *Commission* v *Luxembourg & Belgium* Cases 90 and 91/63 [1964] ECR 625. This case clearly established that under the monist approach, in the event of a conflict between a norm of domestic law and a norm of international law, which produces direct effects in the internal legal system, the treaty rule shall prevail and more specifically that a failure by the Commission to perform one of its obligations to a Member State would not entitle that Member State to suspend its own obligations.

It is recognised in the UK that states do have a duty to ensure that the national laws conform with their treaty obligations so British courts will, when asked to, ensure that the legislature does not violate treaty obligations or generally accepted principles of international law.

The European Communities Act 1972

The legal acts of Community institutions and the jurisprudence of the European Court of Justice and of national law are different in that they break away from the traditional ideas of reciprocal rights and duties as between contracting State parties to an international agreement. In its place an autonomous inherently supreme legal order has been created for the implementation of the objectives of the Treaty of Rome. This legal order is intended to penetrate very deeply into the national legal systems of the Member States.

As was pointed out above, the passage of the European Communities Act 1972 was necessary to give EEC legislation force in the UK. As a result the supreme judicial authority in respect of any legal issue which involves the law of the European Community and British law will be the Court of Justice of the European Community, so in the event of conflict European Community law will prevail and it must be enforced by the British legal system.

The 1972 Act was the legislation which implemented the Treaty of Accession in 1972 and so gave legal effect to the rights and obligations arising from membership of the European Community. The major constitutional objectives of the Act were to be achieved by ss1-3 and the first two Schedules of that Act.

Community treaties to which the Act relates are defined in s1 and Schedule 1. They include, inter alia, the treaty relating to the accession of the United Kingdom to the European Economic Community and to the European Atomic Energy Community (Euratom); the decision of the Council of the European Communities relating to the accession of the United Kingdom to the European Coal and Steel Community and the treaty relating to the accession of the Hellenic Republic to the European Economic Community; to the European Atomic Energy Community; the decision of the Council relating to the accession of the Hellenic Republic to the European Coal and Steel Community; the decision of the Council on the Community system of own resources; the undertaking made by the representatives of the governments of the member states meeting within the Council to make payments to finance the Community's general budget for the financial year 1985; the treaty relating to the accession of the Kingdom of Spain and the Portuguese Republic to the European Economic Community, and the European Atomic Energy Community; the decision of the Council relating to the accession of the Kingdom of Spain and the Portuguese Republic to the European Coal and Steel Community and any other treaty entered into by any of the Communities with or without any of the member states or entered into as a treaty ancillary to any of the treaties by the United Kingdom.

Other treaties may be declared by Order in Council to be Community treaties for the purposes of the Act. Where an Order declares that a treaty entered into by the United Kingdom after 22 January 1972 is such a Community treaty, a draft of the Order must be approved by each House of Parliament s1(3).

The most significant provision of the Act is s2(1) which states:

'All such rights, powers, liabilities, obligations and restrictions from time to time created or arising by or under the treaties, and all such remedies and procedures from time to time provided for by or under the treaties, as in accordance with the treaties are without further enactment to be given legal effect or used in the United Kingdom, shall be recognised and available in law, and be enforced, allowed and followed accordingly; and the expression "enforceable Community right" and similar expressions shall be read as referring to one to which this sub-section applies.'

It can be seen therefore that the operation of Community law within the United Kingdom depends on this sub-section. Through this sub-section all those provisions of Community law which, in accordance with Community law, are directly effective in the United Kingdom are given the force of law. The sub-section will apply to all Community law made either before or after the coming into force of the Act, whether it is contained in Community legislation or in the case law of the Court of Justice.

Section 2(2) also authorises persons entrusted with any statutory power or duty to have regard in exercising it to the objects of the Communities and to Community rights and obligations. The broad effect of this is that Community objectives and Community law may be taken into account where powers are exercised under other UK legislation. This sub-section is expressly stated to be subject to Schedule 2 of the Act which indicates that the powers which are conferred by s2(2) will not include power:

a) to make any provision imposing or increasing taxation;

b) to make any provision taking effect from a date earlier than that of the making of the instrument containing the provision;

c) to confer any power to legislate by means of orders, rules, regulations or other subordinate instrument, other than rules of procedure for any court or tribunal; or

d) to create any new criminal offence punishable with imprisonment for more than two years or punishable on summary conviction with imprisonment for more than three months or with a fine of more than £400 (if not calculated on a daily basis) or with a fine of more than £5 a day.

Section 2(3) indicates that charges on the Consolidated Fund or the National Loans Fund would be made to meet all amounts required to be paid by the UK government to meet its Community obligations, whether to one of the Communities or to other member states. Permanent authority is thus given for such payments and it is unnecessary for Parliament to approve annually of the payment of these sums.

Section 3 refers to decisions on and proof of Community treaties and Community legislation in procedure before UK courts. Section 3(1) indicates that questions as to the meaning of any of the Community treaties, or as to the validity or meaning or effect of any of the Community legislation, shall be treated as questions of law and if not referred to the Court of Justice are to be decided in accordance with the principles laid down by, and relevant decisions of, that Court. The effect of s3(1) fell to be considered by the House of Lords in a criminal trial concerning import controls alleged by the defendants to be contrary to the rules of free movement of goods referred to in articles 30 to 36. The House of Lords held in *R* v *Goldstein* [1983] 1 WLR 151 that:

a) the question of the meaning and effect of articles 30 and 36 was a question of law within the meaning of s3(1) of the European Communities Act 1972 and that accordingly in a criminal trial it was a question for the judge and not for the jury;

b) in view of the express language of s3(1) of that Act it was immaterial at what stage of the legal proceedings a question arose concerning the effect or meaning of any Community instrument and that the question was always to be treated as a question of law.

It was further pointed out that where it is apparent from the outset that a s3(1) question will arise, the most appropriate time to take it is by a motion to quash the indictment before arraignment.

Section 3(2) requires United Kingdom courts to take judicial notice of the Community treaties, the Official Journal of the Communities and of any decision for opinion of the Court of Justice on Community law. The Official Journal shall be admissible as evidence of any instrument or other act thereby communicated of any of the Communities or of any Community institution. The remainder of s3 deals with proof in the United Kingdom courts of instruments issued by Community institutions, including judgments or orders of the Court of Justice.

Other sections made provision for complying with Community rights and obligations, such as s6 which ensured compliance with the Common Agricultural Policy and s9 which ensured compliance with the first directive on harmonisation of company law (now re-enacted elsewhere). Section 11 deals with Community offences, s11(1) makes it an offence in the United Kingdom to give false evidence on oath before the European Court of Justice and s11(2) concerns the disclosure of classified information, particularly in relation to Euratom.

The European Communities (Amendment) Act 1986 has amended the European Communities Act 1972 by including in that Act certain provisions of the Single European Act 1986 (see Chapter 1).

4 Sources of Community Law and Principles of Interpretation

Introduction

The European treaties themselves nowhere define what the sources of Community law are. Unlike the Statute of the International Court of Justice, which enumerates the sources of international law which the Court is called upon to apply, the treaties give instruction to the European Court of Justice in very broad terms only, requiring it to ensure that in the interpretation and application of the treaties 'the law' is observed: article 164.

Community law derives its rules from three broad areas which may be referred to as the primary, secondary, and tertiary sources; these three may be further broken down into seven more specific and readily identifiable sources:

a) Community treaties (primary sources);

b) the acts of the institutions or secondary legislation;

c) Acts adopted by the representatives of the governments of the Member States meeting in Council;

d) the case law of the European Court of Justice;

e) national laws of the Member States;

f) general principles of law; and

g) public international law.

Community treaties

These treaties are those establishing the Communities, as supplemented or amended by other treaties and acts, including the Treaty of Accession. They do not include other treaties concluded by the Member States among themselves relating to the functioning of the Communities or connected with their abilities (eg GATT). Insofar as treaties by the Communities with third States or international organisations are concluded on behalf of the Community by the Council by means of a decision, they fall within the framework of an act of one of its institutions. As such, they form a part of the Community law. In the United Kingdom these various agreements are included in the concept of 'Community treaties' under the European Communities Act 1972 and a special procedure is laid down for the participation of the United Kingdom therein. The Treaties, ECSC, EEC, Euratom are 'self-executing' in that they become law on ratification by the Member States. Generally there is no derogation from the obligations imposed by them, unless grounds for derogation are provided in the Treaty articles as in, for example, article 48 EEC. There is little ground for stating that derogation will be allowed by reference to the principles of international law.

The Treaties define the territorial scope of their application, article 227, but interestingly they have been held to have extra-territorial effect: *Imperial Chemical Industries Ltd* v *EEC Commission* Case 48/69 [1972] CMLR 557 one of the so-called 'dyestuffs' cases where manufacturers with seats outside the community objected to the jurisdiction of the Commission in an anti-competition matter. The court dismissed their objections. The manufacturers were responsible for the activities of subsidiaries within the Community, see also *Béguelin Import* v *SAGL Import-Export* Case 22/71 [1972] CMLR 81.

Acts of the institutions (secondary legislation)

The expression 'secondary legislation' is a collective term comprising all the acts of the two 'law-making' bodies, the Council and Commission, which these two can adopt under the terms of the treaties in their capacity as Community institutions and which create enforceable rights and obligations for Community subjects.

The 'secondary' nature of this legislation implies that it is derived from, limited by, and hierarchically subordinate to the primary sources. This means, in general, that a secondary Community law, whatever its title or nature, cannot legally have the aim and the effect of amending, repealing or altering the scope of a primary treaty provision. It also means, in particular, that the law-making power of the two institutions is subject to three important limitations, non-observance of which entails the invalidity or illegality of the resulting act and renders it liable to annulment by the European Court.

The institutions may act only:

a) in order to carry out their tasks;

b) in accordance with the provisions of the treaties; and

c) within the limits of their respective powers as conferred upon them by the treaties.

These limitations reflect the reluctant transfer of sovereignty from the Member States to the Community institutions. Having considered generally the nature of secondary legislation, the specific acts falling within that description will be considered in turn; article 189 of the Treaty provides:

'In order to carry out their task the Council and the Commission shall, in accordance with the provisions of this treaty make regulations, issue directives, take decisions, make recommendations or deliver opinions.

A regulation shall have general application. It shall be binding in its entirety and directly applicable in all Member States.

A directive shall be binding, as to the result to be achieved, upon each Member State to which it is addressed but shall leave to the national authorities the choice of form and methods.

A decision shall be binding in its entirety upon those to whom it is addressed.'

Recommendations and opinions have no binding force.

a) *Regulations*

In substance regulations are of a truly legislative nature, creating rights and obligations directly and uniformly applicable throughout the whole Community both to the Member States and to individuals within the Member States. They enter into force on the date specified within them or on the twentieth day following publication: article 191(1).

By the express provisions of the treaties, regulations have the following four characteristic features:

i) they are of general application;

ii) they are binding in their entirety;

iii) they are directly applicable; and

iv) they are applicable in all Member States.

i) *General applicability*

It follows from the essentially legislative nature of a regulation that it is applicable not to an individual case or situation, nor to a limited number of defined or identifiable persons, but to objectively determined situations, and involves immediate legal consequences in all the Member States for categories of persons defined in a general and abstract manner.

ii) *Binding in their entirety*

This is what distinguishes a regulation from a directive, which is binding upon the Member State to which it is addressed only as to the result to be achieved while leaving to the national authorities the choice of form and methods. By contrast, Member States must give effect to a regulation in its entirety.

iii) *Direct applicability*

This concept is considered in greater depth later. Briefly, it has three aspects in relation to regulations:

- it is incorporated automatically into the law of each Member State;
- generally speaking it is automatically implemented, although some co-operation may be required from the Member State in carrying out certain specific acts, for example, imposing levies or paying: see *Leonesio* v *Ministerio dell, Agricoltura e Delle Foreste* Case 93/71 [1973] CMLR 343;
- it may create individual rights and obligations, enforceable in the national courts.

iv) *Applicability in all Member States*

Community law requires the simultaneous and uniform application of regulations in all Member States. Consequently, Member States are prohibited from adopting any method of implementation that may jeopardise such application and that would result in a different or discriminatory treatment of the Community citizens according to national criteria.

In addition to these four particular characteristics it follows from the fundamental principle of the supremacy of the Community legal system as a whole that directly applicable provisions of regulations must enjoy the same priority over the national laws of the Member States as directly applicable provisions of the treaty itself enjoy. Two other matters should be noted: (i) article 190 indicates that Regulations (as well as directives and decisions) must be reasoned and failure to comply with this requirement may lead to an annulment action under article 173; and (ii) *Confederation Nationale des Producteurs des Fruits et Legumes* v *Council* Cases 16 and 17/62 [1963] CMLR 160 indicates that the fact that an act is called a regulation is not conclusive as to its status. It was suggested that the substance and not the form *is* conclusive. See also *Greek Canners Association* v *EEC Commission* Case 250/81 [1983] 2 CMLR 32.

b) *Directives*

The EEC Treaty places two different courses of action at the institutions' disposal in order to enable them to carry out the Community's tasks. One is for them to lay down, on direct implementation of the treaties, uniform common rules directly applicable throughout the whole Community. For this the legislative means is the regulation.

The second is to call upon the Member States to exercise their own legislative powers, either for the purpose of adapting their laws to common standards laid down by the institutions, mainly in areas where the diversity of national laws could adversely affect the establishment or functioning of the Common Market, or for the purpose of carrying out the obligations arising from the treaties. For this the legislative form is the directive which accordingly provides an indirect means for the implementation of the treaties.

While a regulation is applicable to Member States and individuals alike, a directive is primarily intended to create legal relationships between the Community and the Member State to which it is addressed. It is binding upon such States, but only as to the result to be achieved, while leaving to the national authorities the choice of form and method. They must be notified to those to whom they are addressed and take effect upon notification: article 191(2).

Generally directives provide no directly enforceable rights for individuals but, as can be seen below, individuals may acquire rights under the directive if the Member State fails to implement the directive within the time limit .

c) *Decisions*

Decisions represent the most versatile and least readily definable form of secondary legislation. The term 'decision' may describe a legally binding measure taken in a specified form and having specific legal effects, as well as a non-binding informal act laying down a programme, a declaration of intention or guidelines which, in order to generate legal effects, must be implemented by further legislative measures. Its most striking feature is that it is binding only upon those to whom it is addressed. A decision therefore is characterised by the limited number of persons, identified or identifiable, to whom it is applicable: article 191(2) above also applies to decisions.

d) *Recommendations and opinions*

Recommendations and opinions differ from regulations, directives and decisions in that, on the one hand, they have no binding force and, on the other, they may be issued by the Council and Commission on any matter dealt with in the treaties at any time when the institutions consider it necessary and not only upon an express authorisation granted in specific cases. Although not binding in law, recommendations and opinions carry considerable political and moral weight.

Acts adopted by the representatives of the governments of the Member States meeting in Council

The Council of the European Communities exercises two different kinds of functions. Primarily, it is a Community institution set up under the treaties and endowed with specific powers and competences.

It is also the setting in which the representatives of the governments of the Member States concentrate their activities and decide on principles and methods of joint action. When acting in its first function, as an organ of the Communities, its measures fall within the concept of 'secondary legislation' (see above).

When meeting as the representatives of the governments of the Member States the Council cannot pass Community measures (as the authority does not arise from the 'basic' treaties). Instead the acts are usually referred to as 'decisions and agreements adopted by the representatives of the governments of the Member States meeting in Council'.

The legal nature of these acts is ambiguous, falling both within Community law (forming a source thereof) and international law. Their nature as international agreements between sovereign states - albeit dealing with Community-related subject matter - generally prevents acts being subject to the European Court's judicial review.

However, the court has attributed to decisions of the representatives of the Member States the same legislative effect as a decision of the Council qua Community institution, in *Luxembourg* v *European Parliament* Case 230/81 [1983] CMLR 726, where Luxembourg challenged the Parliament's decision to establish its seat in Strasbourg and Brussels.

The advantage of this form of decision-making is that it provides a quick and simple way for the Member States to take action in areas outside Community competences. At the same time, it has the disadvantage of enabling the Council to take action in disregard to the conditions and procedures laid down by the treaties in situations where in reality it might have acted as a Community institution, and this might upset the institutional balance within the Communities.

The case law of the European Court of Justice

Unlike the position in the common law countries, in the Continental civil law systems the doctrine of the binding force of precedents does not apply. Since the European Court is modelled upon the Continental courts, it is generally not bound by its own previous decisions. The context of the binding force of the Court's judgment is governed instead by the principle concerning res judicata. According to this principle a judgment's binding effect is only relative and exists only insofar as there is an identity of parties, cause and subject matter.

Consequently, it is from the moral authority of its decisions rather than from the legal authority that the Court's case law derives its force. Strictly speaking, therefore, the case law of the European Court cannot be regarded as a formal source of law.

However, in the first place, it may be expected that wherever the Court has given a leading judgment it will be unlikely to depart from it in subsequent cases without strong reasons, even though it retains the right to do so. Certainly, the case law of the European Court over the quarter of a century of its existence reveals a remarkable consistency of adjudication on both substantive and procedural issues. (See *Procureur de la Republique* v *Chiron* Case 271-274/84 [1988] 1 CMLR 735.)

In the second place, wherever the Court interprets a provision, clarifies a concept, or defines a rule, its judgment inescapably has an effect going beyond the individual case.

Finally, the Court has as a matter of fact often ventured into a form of legislation; for example, by recognising the community's treaty-making power in the field of transport, or by extending the concept of a prohibited abuse by undertakings of a dominant position to mergers.

National laws of the Member States

The division between the national and Community powers and competences inevitably prevents the national laws of the Member States from forming a formal source of Community law. Nevertheless, there are two specific situations where the court does apply, or at least calls upon, rules and concepts of municipal law.

a) Where Community law expressly or by implication refers to the laws of the Member States. This is normally the case where the nationality, personal status or legal capacity of individuals, or the status, legal capacity or representation of legal persons or of entities without legal personality, is in question. The question whether the condition is fulfilled is decided by the application of the relevant municipal law: *Wilhelm* v *Bundeskartellamt* Case 14/68 [1969] ECR 103.

b) Where Community law has developed in the legal systems of the Member States the European Court turns for guidance to the laws of those States, particularly where there is a gap in Community law.

General principles of law

Except for the single case of non-contractual liability, article 215, the European Court is not directed by any explicit treaty provision to apply the 'general principles of law' in deciding disputes submitted to it.

However, it is generally recognised that 'the law' which the Court is directed to apply includes the general principles of law of the legal systems of the Member States which the Court will incorporate into the common law of the Communities. A number of such general principles of law have been recognised including:

Protection of fundamental human rights: in *Stauder* v *City of Ulm* Case 29/69 [1970] CMLR 112 an article 177 reference was made by a German court which was hearing a claim that a Community measure involved an infringement of fundamental human rights. The ECJ gave an interpretation which was consistent with the principles of Community law and the protection of fundamental human rights, an implicit acknowledgement which was followed by the explicit formulation in *Internationale Handelsgesellschaft* Case 11/70 [1970] CMLR 255 where in the course of judgment it was stated that ' ... respect for fundamental human rights forms an integral part of general principles of law protected by the Court of Justice. The protection of such rights, while inspired by the constitutional traditions common to the Member States, must be ensured within the framework of the structure and objectives of the Community'. To the 'constitutional traditions', 'international treaties for the protection of human rights' were added as guidelines which should be followed: *Nold* v *Commission* Case 4/73 [1974] 2 CMLR 338. This was obviously a reference to the European Convention for the Protection of Human Rights and Fundamental Freedoms to which all Member States are parties. See *R* v *Kirk* Case 63/83 [1984] CMLR 522 for an example of the application of the ECHR (article 7) in an article 177 referral.

Legal certainty: in *Da Costa en Shaake* v *Nederlandse Belasting Administratie* Cases 28-30/62 [1963] CMLR, Advocate-General M Lagrange stated, 'The rule that res judicata binds only the particular case is the weapon which permits the court to do this (alter its view of the law). Of course they should only use this weapon prudently, on pain of destroying legal certainty...' - so establishing legal certainty as one of the general principles of community law. The principle was invoked by the court in *Defrenne* v *Sabena* Case 43/75 [1976] CMLR 98 as a major ground for refusing to allow retrospective direct effect to article 119.

The principle would appear to embody the concept of respect for legitimate expectations and the principle that Community measures may not have retroactive effect, *Council* v *Parliament* Case 34/86 [1986] 3 CMLR 94, and *R* v *Kirk* above. It must be noted, however, that where the purpose to be achieved demands it and where the legitimate expectations of concerned parties are respected a measure may be held to be retroactive: *Decker* v *Hauptzollampt Landau* Case 99/78 [1979] ECR 101 and *Amylum* v *Council* Case 108/81 [1982] ECR 3107.

Proportionality: this principle involves the notion that administrative measures must be proportionate to the aim to be achieved. First mooted in the *Internationale Handelsgesellschaft* case and taken further in *Balkan Imp-Exp GmbH* v *Hauptzallampt Berlin-Packhof* Case 5/73 [1973] ECR 1091 and some of the so-called Isoglucose cases. These cases involved an indirect challenge to regulations which imposed levies on the producers of *Isoglucose*, a form of sugar substitute - there was a surplus of sugar on the market: *Royal Scholten Honig* v *IBAP* Cases 103 & 145/77 [1978] ECR 2037 where it was found that the levy was excessive and disproportionate as it had the effect of driving the producer from the market thereby eliminating competition.

The principle has been applied also in other than purely economic areas. In *Lynne Watson and Alessandro Belmann* Case 118/75 [1976] ECR 1185 it was found that the suggested deportation of Watson from Italy by the authorities was a measure disproportionate to the crime committed, that was, failure to comply with administrative requirements. The conclusion of the Court was also an illustration of the jealousy with which the Court regards basic rights given by the Treaty, here the right of free movement of workers under article 48.

Equality: equality was acknowledged in *Ferrario* Case 152/81 [1983] ECR 2357 as one of the basic principles of community law. Its application may be seen most frequently in cases involving discrimination on grounds of gender (*Sabbatini* v *Parliament* Case 20/71 [1972] CMLR 945) and religion (*Prais* v *Council* Case 130/75 [1976] 2 CMLR 708).

Legal professional privilege: in *AM & S Europe Ltd* v *Commission* Case 155/79 [1982] ECR 1575 it was acknowledged that the principle whereby written communications between lawyer and client are privileged would be upheld. The principle is however confined to those communications between an independent lawyer and his/her client and does not extend to in-house lawyers or lawyers from non-member States.

Note should be made of the decision in *National Panasonic (UK) Ltd* v *Commission* Case 136/79 [1980] 3 CMLR 169 where the right to privacy cannot be upheld if it serves to thwart the enforcement of Community Competition Law.

Public international law

The extent to which public international law may be regarded as a source of Community law is determined by the dual nature of the European Communities as, on the one hand, entities established by treaties under international law and, on the other hand, autonomous bodies with quasi-sovereign powers creating their own autonomous legal order which is distinct from both international and national law.

This first aspect implies that, to the extent to which the Communities possess legal personality under international law, they are in principle subject to the rules of that law. Thus it is international law that governs their external relations, whether treaty or other relations with third countries and international organisations, as in the exercise of their external powers (eg treaty-making power), and of their internal powers with an external effect, the Communities must conform with public international law. As such it forms part of the 'law', the observance of which it is the task of the European Court to ensure.

Principles of interpretation

The obvious need for judicial interpretation of legal texts has developed certain rules and methods of interpretation in all national, international and supranational courts. The difference is in accentuating one or other of these methods, depending on the nature of the text to be interpreted and on the legal system in which the interpretation is to take place.

Generally speaking, three principal methods of interpretation may be distinguished, whose aim is to discover, respectively:

a) the objective meaning of the words actually used, in the context of the instrument as a whole (grammatico-logical and systematic interpretation);

b) the subjective intention of the legislator or, in the case of a contract/treaty, the common intention of the contracting parties (historical interpretation); and

c) the object and purpose of the particular provision as well as the instrument as a whole (teleological interpretation).

The general pattern of interpretation followed by the European Court is to examine in turn the wording, general scheme and spirit of the provision in question as well as its position in the system of the Treaty and its role in the light of the Treaty's objectives.

Where the provision is an act of secondary legislation it is examined in the light of the spirit, system and objectives of both the Act itself and the relevant treaty provisions under which the Act was adopted.

The first step in the process of interpretation is to examine the wording of the provision in question. Since no preparatory work has been made public in respect of the basic Community treaties which would clearly express the intention of the Member States, the Court usually bases its interpretation upon the text in the form in which it has been drafted and gives it the significance which flows naturally from, or comes as close as reasonably possible to, the literal and logical meaning of the words.

Generally, where upon examination of its wording the Court finds that a provision is absolutely clear and unequivocal, no further interpretation is necessary. The text may then be applied as it stands. Where, however, literal interpretation fails to give a definite answer or leads to a conclusion which runs counter to common sense, to the basic principles of Community law or to its rational application, the Court looks beyond the text to equity, the 'spirit of the law', and, to a lesser extent, to the real or presumed intention of the legislator.

Perhaps most importantly, a provision is interpreted according to its position in the system of the Treaty (systematic interpretation) and in the light of its own, as well as the Treaty's, purposes and objects (teleological interpretation). In the practice of the European Court these two methods appear as two sides of the same coin and are therefore usually employed simultaneously. They represent a dominant, and without doubt the most characteristic, feature of the Court's own particular way of interpretation.

This method of interpretation is based on a combination of two general propositions:

a) in principle, the provisions of a treaty must be read together and, insofar as possible, reconciled with one another, since they mutually complement and supplement each other; and

b) the introductory articles to a treaty lay down obligatory general principles and objectives whose pursuit is indispensable for the achievement of the relevant Community's tasks. Their scope of application extends over the whole spectrum of that treaty and consequently they are decisive for the interpretation of those more detailed provisions which give effect to them.

In practice, the use made by the Court of Justice of the various methods of interpretation discussed above is subordinate to the operation of three fundamental principles of overriding importance. These principles are designed to ensure that the specific supranational nature of the

Community's legal system is duly taken into account, and given effect to, in the interpretation of its individual provisions. These are the principles of:

a) uniformity;

b) effectiveness, and

c) protection of individual rights.

The principle of uniformity

The requirement of uniform interpretation and application of Community law throughout the Member States is essential to the autonomous and supranational character of Community law.

It follows that undefined terms appearing in Community texts which are also used in the national laws of the Member States (eg 'worker', 'public policy') must be presumed to have an independent Community meaning which must prevail over any different or conflicting meaning attributed to them in other legal systems. They must therefore be interpreted according to independent Community criteria, ie by reference, in the first place, to the scheme, object and purpose of the Community text in which they occur and, in the second place, to the general principles of Community law.

The principle of uniformity further requires that Community texts of general application (eg regulations or directives and decisions addressed to the Member States) should be interpreted in the light of their versions in the official language of the Communities. All these versions being equally binding, no single one of them can be regarded as the solely authentic text. In cases of divergences between the various translations, an attempt must be made to derive a meaning common to them all from the scheme, object and purpose of the provision. In the absence of such a meaning, preference must be given to the interpretation that is least onerous for Community subjects, provided that it suffices to achieve the purpose covered by the text. This is on the assumption that the legislator did not intend to impose stricter obligations or confer less rights in some of the Member States than in others.

The principle of effectiveness

This principle has the effect that, where there are various alternatives, preference must be given to an interpretation that tends to prevent the effectiveness or validity of basic Community rules being undermined.

Therefore, the various exceptions and obligations allowed by the

Treaty in such fundamental provisions as, for example, those relating to the free movement of workers must be interpreted and applied restrictively.

Also, since in principle integration under the EEC Treaty is of a comprehensive character, and is not to take place separately according to economic sectors, particular provisions relating to individual sectors must be interpreted narrowly by reason of their exceptional nature.

Finally, the principle of effectiveness enables such implied powers to be attributed to the Community institutions as are necessary for a proper and effective implementation of the provisions of the Treaties.

The principle of the protection of individual rights

This principle applies to the interpretation of both substantive and procedural provisions of Community law.

In the context of substantive law, it applies so that where a provision is silent or obscure it must be given a meaning that is the least unfavourable to individuals, ie it affords to them the widest possible freedom of action that is still compatible with Community interests in general and with the purpose of that provision in particular.

Similarly, with regard to procedural requirements, the provisions of the treaties enabling individuals to bring actions in the European Court in defence or enforcement of their substantive Community rights should not be interpreted restrictively to the detriment of the person concerned. This obviously does not result in an interpretation which would disregard the clear limitations placed by the Treaties on the system that they have created for the legal protection of individuals.

5 Direct Applicability and Direct Effect

Introduction
Direct applicability and direct effect: definition
The limits of direct effect

Introduction

It is necessary to ascertain the extent to which the law of the European Community confers rights and duties on individuals and it is in this context that the above expressions will be examined. The difficulties which beset this exercise were outlined by President Lecourt who stated that: 'either the Community, for individuals, is a fascinating but distant abstraction, of concern only to Governments, which apply its rules at their discretion; or else it is an effective reality for them and therefore a creator of legal rights and duties.'

L'Europe des Juges; Brussels 1976. If the Member States are the addressees of all the rights and duties deriving from the Treaties, then an individual's rights and duties would not be derived from those sources but from national legislation which the Member States had adopted in pursuit of their obligations under the Treaties. A cordon sanitaire would therefore exist between national and Community Law, a position previously asserted by the Member States. The starting point for any study of how the law affects individuals is article 177:

'The Court of Justice shall have jurisdiction to give preliminary rulings concerning:

a) the interpretation of this Treaty;

b) the validity and interpretation of acts of the institutions of the Community;

c) the interpretation of the statutes of bodies established by an act of the Council, where these statutes so provide.

Where such a question is raised before any court or tribunal of a Member State that court or tribunal may, if it considers that a decision on the question is necessary to enable it to give judgment, request the Court of Justice to give a ruling thereon.

Where such a question is raised on a case pending before a court or tribunal of a Member State, against whose decisions there is no judicial remedy under national law, that court or tribunal shall bring the matter before the Court of Justice.'

Preliminary rulings are given by the European Court of Justice in response to questions referred to it by national courts or tribunals concerning the interpretation of the Treaties and acts of the institutions or the validity of the acts of the institutions. They are essentially in the nature of an interim step in an action which has been started in a national court and in which the substantive issues will be settled by the same court in the light of the rulings of the European Court. The primary purpose of preliminary rulings is thus to enable national courts to reach decisions in cases properly brought before them but in which the decision depends on the prior clarification of legal issues falling within the jurisdiction of the European court.

NV Algemene Transport-en Expeditie Onderneming Van Gend en Loos v *Nederlandse Tariefcommissie* Case 26/62 [1963] CMLR 105

In November 1960 the company imported from Germany some chemical product. At the date of importation the product was classified within a certain technical group, the Dutch authorities imposed a duty of 8 per cent whereas the other products within that group were subject only to 3 per cent duty. On appeal to the Amsterdam Tax Court the Dutch Revenue Authorities stated that an even higher impost was due. The Tax Court referred the matter to the European Court to determine two preliminary questions which were: could a citizen of a Member State enforce individual rights which should be protected by that state and, was the duty imposed illegal in the light of the provisions of article 12? (Article 12 provides that Member States should refrain from imposing new customs duties or increasing existing ones).

The Court, in a lengthy judgment, outlined the 'new legal order' which the Treaty had created and substantiated its position by stating that to find out if the provisions of an International Treaty have immediate effect in domestic law it is necessary to look at 'the spirit, the general scheme and the wording of those provisions.' The Court further pointed out that the Treaty objective was to establish a common market the functioning of which was of 'direct concern to the interested parties in the Community' which implied that the Treaty was more than an agreement creating mutual obligations between contracting Member States. This contention is interlinked with a major Treaty objective, the elimination of obstacles to the free movement of goods, article 3. Community law should therefore match this objective.

The Court was also much exercised by the fact that other matters in the objects of the Treaty and indeed other Treaty provisions ensured that individuals were to be concerned directly in Community law. Their opinion was that Community law was a new legal order within which Member States have limited their sovereign rights, in certain areas, and the subjects of this law were not only the States but also their nationals: 'the Community has its own institutions, independent of the Member States, with power to issue legal regulations which directly created rights and obligations not only for the Member States themselves but also for nationals of those States.'

The Court applied the above principles to the case before it and decided that article 12 contained a clear prohibition which was not a positive but a negative obligation to which there was no reservation making it dependent on domestic law for its implementation. The conclusion reached was that the article had direct effect and created individual rights which the national courts had to protect. The Court's judgment here followed a judgment handed down in the *Italian Consiglio di Stato, Societa Biscotti Panettoni Colussi di Milano* v *Ministero del Commercio con L'Estero* Case 778 [1963] CMLR 133 where it was held that article 31 was directly effective.

In *Van Gend en Loos* the Court had to devote a large portion of their judgment to outlining what was meant by this new order because it wished not only to answer the submissions that direct effect was an exception but also to emphasise that the individual is affected by Community law and that the existence of the procedures under articles 169 and 170, for obtaining a declaration of default, did not imply that it was impossible for individuals in appropriate cases before a national court to rely on the Member State's obligations. The Court stated that 'a restriction of the guarantee against an infringement of article 12 by Member States to the procedures under articles 169 and 170 would remove all direct legal protection of the individual rights of their nationals. There is a risk that recourse to the procedure under these articles would be ineffective if it were to occur after the implementation of a national decision taken contrary to the provisions of the Treaty ... the vigilance of individuals concerned to protect their rights amounts to an effective supervision in addition to the supervision entrusted by articles 169 and 170 to the diligence of the Commission and the Member States.'

Direct applicability and direct effect: definition

Direct applicability is a description of the quality which enables a provision of Community law to become a part of the national law of a Member State without the necessity of legislation; ie it is incorporated directly in the corpus of national law; see article 189 and its reference to the direct applicability of regulations

Direct effect means that a provision of Community law can be interpreted by the Court as being able to create rights which any natural or legal person may enforce against the state and sometimes against other persons. The right once established must be protected by the national courts, see *Amsterdam Bulb BV* v *Productschap voor Siergewassen* Case 50/76 [1977] ECR 137; *Van Gend en Loos* v *Nederlandse Tariefcommissie* Case 26/62 [1963] CMLR 105 and article 189, SZ(1) European Communities Act 1972.

Although the Court use the terms invariably, it is proposed in the following discussion to adhere approximately to the definitions above. The two qualities will be discussed in relation to the various types of Community law.

Treaty articles

It was stated above that among the factors enabling the European Court of Justice to reach their historic judgment in *Van Gend en Loos* was the fact that article 12 contained a negative obligation. This element of the Court's reasoning gave rise to a belief that the test for determining the direct effect of a Treaty article was whether it was a prohibition or not. The rigidity of such a test has been mitigated somewhat by subsequent cases to the extent that the test has been stated to be that the provision in question must be: clear and unambiguous; unconditional and must not depend on subsequent legislation of the Community or national authorities and must not lead to the latter having an effective power of discretionary judgment as to the application of the provision in question, see *Molkerei-Zentrale Westfalen/Lippe GmbH* v *Hauptzollampt Paderborn* Case 28/67 [1968] ECR 143 and *Reyners* v *Belgium* Case 2/74 [1974] ECR 631.

It is instructive to observe the conclusions of the Court in the cases from *Van Gend en Loos* onwards. The famous case of *Costa* v *Ente Nazionale per l'Energia Elettrica* (ENEL) Case 6/64 [1964] CMLR 425 concerned rather complex arguments which need not be fully recited here but it suffices to say that the Court was given the opportunity to pronounce on four Treaty articles and their direct effect. Article 37(2), which concerns the introduction of new measures dealing with the abolition of customs duties and quantitative restrictions, was held to confer individual rights to which the national courts must give effect, see also *Francesco Cinzano & Cia GmbH* v *Hauptzollampt, Saarbruecken* Case 13/70 [1971] CMLR 374. Article 53, dealing with restrictions on the right of establishment, was also held to be directly effective; articles 93, state aids and 102, concerning consultation with the Commission in matters relating to amendments by Member State of Community provisions, were held not to be. The Court followed the *Van Gend en Loos* 'clear prohibition' line of reasoning and did so again in the case of *Salgoil SpA* v *Foreign Trade Ministry of the Italian Republic* Case 13/68 [1969] CMLR 181, which concerned the import of fat-impregnated bleaching earth from Switzerland. The Court held that provisions of the Treaty which impose a clear and unqualified obligation on Member States and which require no further action for their implementation are directly effective. Articles 31, quantitative restrictions and 32(1), under the terms of which the Member States in their trade with each other shall refrain from making more restrictive the quotas and measures having equivalent effect existing at the date of the entry into force of the Treaty, accordingly were directly effective. It should be noted from the above cases that the Court was determining the cases with an eye on the major Treaty objectives.

In a judgment handed down between the two cases above, the court showed flexibility in their approach to defining a prohibition. *Alfons Lutticke* v *Hauptzollampt Saarlouis* Case 57/65 [1966] ECR 205, which concerned the imposition of customs duties and equalisation tax on powdered milk imported from Luxembourg into Germany, dealt with article 95. The article forbids any discriminatory internal taxation on imported products similar to 95(1), or competing with, 95(2), national products, 95(3) indicates that 'Member States shall not later than at the beginning of the second stage, repeal or amend any provisions existing when this Treaty enters into force which conflict with the preceding rules.' It was held that 95(1) imposed a prohibition against discrimination which amounted to a clear and unconditional obligation and therefore had direct effect. The Court held that 95(3) imposed an obligation on Member States which did not leave them any discretion as to the date by which they had to repeal or amend contrary provisions; the obligation clearly had to be fulfilled by 1 January 1962. 'After this date it is sufficient for the national court to find, should the case arise, that the measures implementing the contested national rules of law were adopted after 1 January 1962 in order to be able to apply the first paragraph directly in any event.' The judgment seems to make it clear that an obligation to act, here by repeal or amending, is transformed into an obligation to refrain from imposing contrary provisions after the expiry of the period fixed for fulfilling the positive obligation.

The consequences of the view taken by the Court in *Lutticke* can be seen in the Court's treatment of article 8(7) and the cases concerning the rights of establishment and the free movement of goods. Article 8(7) provides that, 'Save for the exceptions or derogations provided for in this Treaty, the expiry of the transitional period shall constitute the latest date by which all the rules laid down must enter into force and all the measures required for establishing the common market must be implemented.' Indeed it is safe to say that the more important articles concerning the free movement of goods which are clear and unconditional are now directly effective; articles 9, 16, 30 and 95.

Articles 52-58 deal with the right of establishment and they provide, inter alia, that restrictions on the right of establishment shall be abolished 'by progressive stages in the course of the transitional period', article 52, by means of directives which were to be adopted by the Council in the implementation of a general programme, article 54. In addition the Council was, by means of directives issued during the same period, to give effect to mutual recognition of diplomas, certificates and other qualifications and to co-ordinate the rules under which persons take up and pursue activities as self-employed persons, article 57.

At the end of the transitional period, no directives had been adopted regarding certain professional activities; these included the legal profession. In a preliminary ruling on a question referred by the Belgian Conseil d'Etat in the case of *Reyners* v *Belgium* Case 2/74 [1974] ECR 631, which concerned a Dutch national who lived in Belgium who had the necessary Belgian qualifications but was prevented from practising because Belgian law only allowed Belgian nationals to be admitted to practice, it was held that article 52(2) had had direct effect since 1 January 1970. The Court pointed out that in laying down that freedom of establishment shall be attained at the end of the transitional period, article 52 thereby imposes an obligation to obtain a precise result, the fulfilment of which had to be made easier by, but not dependent on, the implementation of a programme of progressive measures. The fact that this progression has not been adhered to leaves the obligation itself intact beyond the end of the period provided for its fulfilment.

This interpretation is 'in accordance' with article 8(7) of the Treaty. All of which implies that any directives adopted in the future would not be intended to implement the rule on equal treatment with nationals. This rule has been effective since January 1970 by virtue of article 52 and the the right to free establishment.

As a result of this judgment, the Commission withdrew a number of proposals for directives in order to concentrate its attention on co-ordinating conditions of taking up and pursuit of the professions.

The conclusion to be drawn from *Reyners* case is that article 52 was not only directly effective but also directly applicable. The Court held that the same effect occurred at the end of the transitional period in the case of article 37(1). The article deals with the progressive adjustment of State monopolies of a commercial character. The judgment in *Pubblico Ministero* v *Flavia Manghera* Case 59/75 [1976] ECR 91 pointed out that:

'the fact that at the end of the transitional period no discrimination regarding the conditions under which goods are procured and marketed must exist between nationals of Member States constitutes an obligation with a very precise objective, subject to a clause postponing its operation. Upon the expiry of the transitional period this obligation is no longer subject to any condition or contingent in its execution or in its effects, upon the introduction of any measure, either by the Community or by the Member States and by its nature it is capable of being relied on by nationals of Member States before national courts.'

A further illustration of this line is to be found in the case of *Iannelli and Volpi SpA* v *Meroni* Case 74/76 [1977] ECR 557 which dealt with article 30. It was held that:

'the prohibition of quantitative restrictions and measures having equivalent effect ... is mandatory and its implementation does not require any subsequent intervention of the Member States or Community institutions. The prohibition therefore has direct effect and creates individual rights which the national courts must protect; this occurred at the end of the transitional period at the latest, that is to say on 1 January 1970, as the provisions of the second paragraph of article 32 of the Treaty indicate.'

It may be tentatively suggested that the judgments in the above cases show that the Court is intent on making up for the failure of the national authorities and the Community institutions to complete the task set for them for the transitional period under the Treaty.

The cases so far have dealt with the right of an individual to invoke against his/her state, before a national court, the effects arising from an obligation imposed on the Member States by the Treaty; this is called the vertical effect of a provision.

Some provisions, because of their nature, have been recognised by the Court as having a wider effect in that those provisions can be invoked against other individuals: this is known as a horizontal effect in that they impose obligations on other individuals.

The Treaty provisions regarding the competition rules applicable to undertakings can clearly be invoked before the national courts by one undertaking against another, see *Robert Bosch GmbH* v *de Geus* Case 13/61 [1962] CMLR 1, which concerned a sole agency agreement in Holland to distribute Bosch products.

The provisions dealing with the free movement of persons certainly give an individual rights which can be invoked in a dispute with national authorities, *Commission* v *France* Case 167/73 [1974] ECR 359 where the Court had to decide on article 48 of the Treaty and its application to the facts of the case which concerned a French law restricting certain occupations on board French registered ships, to French nationals. The Court held that the article was directly applicable so its application could extend to agreements and rules which did not emanate from national authorities. A proposition which found an echo in the case of *Walrave and Koch* v *Association Union Cycliste Internationale* Case 36/74 [1975] CMLR 320. The case concerned the rules of the union which provided that in world championship races which took place behind a pacer on a motorbike the pacer had to be of the same nationality as his stayer. The Court stated that, 'the activities referred to in article 59 are not distinguished by their nature from those in article 48 ... it follows that the provisions of articles 7, 48 and 59 of the Treaty can be taken into account by the national court ... ' (in an action against a sporting organisation).

Article 119 which provides that, 'each Member State shall during the first stage ensure and subsequently maintain the application of the principle that men and women receive equal pay for equal work ...' has been held to apply 'not only to the action of public authorities, but also extends to all agreements which are intended to regulate paid labour collectively as well as contracts between individuals. *Defrenne* v *SA Sabena* Case 43/75 [1976] ECR 455 a case which provided the Court with an opportunity to widen its view on direct application. Whereas in *Walrave* the Court had relied on 'the general nature of the terms of article 59, which makes no distinction between the source of the restrictions to be abolished', in *Defrenne* the Court held that article 119 imposed on Member States, 'a duty to bring about a specific result to be mandatorily achieved within a fixed period' and the reference to Member States 'cannot be interpreted as excluding the intervention of the Courts in direct application of the Treaty.'

This horizontal effect giving rights to individuals inter se which the Court has accorded to some Treaty provisions, gives a new scope to 'direct effect' as it has been generally understood since *Van Gend en Loos*.

There are, of course, provisions to which the Court has refused to accord direct effect. A review of these cases is worthwhile in order to determine more precisely, a contrario, the criteria on which this effect is based.

In its judgment in *Costa* v *ENEL* the Court refused to accord direct effect to articles 102 and 93, except for the last sentence of article 93(3).

Article 102 obliges the Member States to consult the Commission when there is reason to fear that a provision laid down by law may cause 'distortion of competition'. In the Court's view the States have thereby contracted with the Community an undertaking 'which binds them as States, but which does not create individual rights which national courts must protect'. Similarly in agreeing to notify the Commission within a reasonable time of their aid projects and in agreeing to submit to the procedures laid down in article 93, the States have entered into an obligation which the Court describes in the same words which are used in the case of article 102, 'except in the case of the final provision of article 93(3), which is not in question in the present case'.

The last sentence of article 93(3) forbids the State to grant aid before the Commission has completed the procedure for reviewing the project. It used to be thought, on the basis of these cases, that purely procedural obligations imposed on the States only concerned the relations between the States and the Community and therefore had no direct effect.

However, nine years later, in the judgment in *Lorenz* v *Germany* Case 120/73 [1973] ECR 1471, the Court cited its earlier judgment and pointed out that the immediately applicable character of a prohibition (on implementing a project to grant aid) extends to the whole of the period to which it applies: 'Thus the direct effect of the prohibition extends to all aid which has been implemented without being notified and, in the event of notification, operates during the preliminary period, and where the Commission sets in motion the contentious procedure up to the final decision.' It is clear, therefore, that an individual can rely before a court on the failure to notify the Commission of a new aid.

On the other hand the Court does not recognise the individual as having a right to claim that an existing aid is contrary to the Treaty.

This is because the 'incompatibility of aid with the Common Market is neither absolute nor unconditional'. The Court points out that not only are exceptions provided for but that both article 92 and article 93 confer a wide discretionary power on the Commission and give the Council extensive power to allow State aid, by way of exception to the general prohibition contained in article 92(1), and it draws the conclusion that:

'It is the intention of the Treaty... that the finding that an aid may be incompatible with the Common Market is to be determined, subject to review by the Court, by means of an appropriate procedure which it is the Commission's responsibility to set in motion,' *Ianelli* (see above).

It was once again the existence of a discretionary power, this time residing not in the institutions but in the Member States, on which the Court relied when refusing direct effect to articles 32 (last sentence) and 33 dealing with tariff quotas, *Salgoil,* and 97 dealing with the States' option to establish average rates in order to remedy the discriminatory character of certain cascade taxes, *Molkerei-Zentrale.* These cases have lost their importance because of the expiry of the transitional period, in the first case, and the imposition of value added tax (VAT) to replace cascade tax, in the second. But the criterion applied, namely the existence of a discretionary power, still holds good.

This last line of cases seems to put the emphasis on the developing character of direct effect. The action of the institutions gives form to provisions which in themselves are purely in the nature of a programme. In this connection some judgments may be mentioned dealing with the Community's monetary powers. The Court was asked whether articles 5 and 107 of the Treaty together with the resolution adopted by the Council and the representatives of the governments of the Member States on 22 March 1971 regarding the realisation, in stages, of economic and monetary union, ought to have been interpreted as forbidding the Member states to allow their currencies to float. After pointing out that:

'One of the cardinal aims of the Treaty is the creation of a single economic region, free from internal restrictions, in which the customs union and the economic union may be progressively achieved', that this objective requires fixed exchange rates between the currencies and that: 'Article 3(g) provides for the procedures to be followed in order to co-ordinate the economic policies of the Member States and to remedy any disequilibria in their balance of payments', the Court states that until the procedures envisaged by this provision have been put into operation articles 5 and 107 allow the Member States, despite the duty imposed on each of them to regard its policy on rates of exchange as a matter of common concern, such freedom of decision that the obligation contained in these articles 5 and 107 cannot confer on interested parties rights which the national courts would be bound to protect. *Schluter* v *Hauptzollampt Lorrach* Case 9/73 [1973] ECR 1135.

This line of reasoning can be assimilated to the grounds of its judgment adopted by the Court in *Defrenne* on article 119 regarding equal pay for men and women. In *Defrenne* the Court distinguished between direct discrimination which can be found to exist simply by virtue of the criteria contained in article 119 ('equal pay for equal work') and indirect discrimination which can be only combated by means of appropriate Community and national measures. In the view of the Court, the prohibition of direct discrimination at all events is directly applicable. In *Defrenne* it states that in the absence of provisions implementing articles 117 and 118, it cannot interpret article 119 as extending beyond equal pay to cover equal working conditions.

It is clear that although the Court makes up for failures on the part of the institutions and the States by giving direct effect to provisions when the period within which they should have been implemented has expired, it sets limits to this procedure by refusing to accord this effect to provisions which it considers too general and indeterminate a scope for any clear rules to be inferred. (See below the discussion concerning directives).

Regulations

Article 189(2) of the Treaty reads as follows: 'A regulation shall have general application. It shall be binding in its entirety and directly applicable in all Member States.' As law 'per se' a regulation is capable of both horizontal and vertical effect (see above) which means that regulations can impose obligations on individuals as well as the state. Observe the formula from the case of *Politi* v *Italian Ministry of Finance* Case 43/71 [1971] ECR 1039. In dealing with article 189(2) the Court recognised that, 'by reason of their nature and their function in the system of the sources of Community law, regulations have direct effect and are, as such, capable of creating individual rights which national courts must protect.' A note of warning must be sounded here as direct applicability does not necessarily mean directly effective for it was pointed out by Roemer AG in the case of *Leonesio* v *Italian Ministry of Agriculture and Forestry* Case 93/71 [1972] ECR 287, that the exact legal effect of a provision will depend on whether an implementation discretion was left to national authorities and to what extent the provision had to be completed by national provisions. See also *Gemeenschappelijke Verzekeringskas 'de Sociale Voorzorg'* v *WH Bertholet* Case 31/64 [1966] CMLR 191. Many of the cases in this area dealt with provisions in regulations for the organisation of the agricultural markets with a similar content to the contents of the Treaty provisions pertaining to the customs union which the Court recognised as having direct effect.

The *Leonesio* judgment is instructive (cited above). Signora Leonesio, a farmer, had slaughtered some cattle and unsuccessfully claimed from the State the payment of a premium to which she was entitled under Community regulations. The Italian State in its defence claimed that under article 81 of the constitution it was bound to adopt a law in order to effect the payment of the disputed premium. It was held by the Court that once the conditions laid down in the regulations were satisfied upon expiry of the period fixed for establishing proof of slaughter, 'the above mentioned regulations give the farmer the right to require payment of the subsidy without that Member State being able to rely on arguments based on any legislative provisions or administrative practices to withhold such payment ... so as to apply with equal force with regard to nationals of all the Member States, Community regulations become part of the legal system applicable within the national territory which must permit the direct effect provided for in article 189 to operate in such a way that reliance thereon by individuals may not be frustrated by domestic provisions or practices. Budgetary provisions of a Member State cannot therefore hinder the direct applicability of a Community provision and consequently the exercise of individual rights created by such a provision.'

It is noteworthy that the Court recognises the primacy of a regulation over budgetary powers contained in the constitution. It is of course firmly in agreement with the line taken by the Court in *Costa* v *Enel*. Note, however, that the case dealt with the implementation of rules which did not require action by the state.

Directives

Directives defined in article 189 as 'binding as to the result to be achieved upon each member state to which it is addressed but shall leave to the national authorities choice of form and methods', are not directly applicable but may have 'vertical' direct effect.

In the case of *Franzgrad* v *Finanzampt Traustein* Case 9/70 [1970] ECR 825 the Court gave judgment on the combined effect of a decision that value added tax was incompatible with other turnover taxes and the directive instituting VAT.

It held that: 'Although it is true that by virtue of Article 189, regulations are directly applicable and therefore by virtue of their nature capable of producing direct effects, it does not follow from this that other categories of legal measures mentioned in that article can never produce similar effects ...'. It would be incompatible with the binding effect attributed to decisions by article 189 to exclude in principle the possibility that persons affected may invoke the obligations imposed by a decision. Particularly in cases where, for example, the Community authorities by means of a decision have imposed an obligation of a Member State or all the Member States to act in a certain way, the effectiveness, l'effet utile, of such a measure would be weakened if the nationals of that State could not take it into consideration as part of Community law.

It is clear that the Court connected its conclusions as to direct effect of acts other than regulations with considerations based on their effectiveness, in complete accord with the relationship established, since the *Van Gend en Loos* judgment, between direct effect and the efficacy of Community law.

In the *Sace* v *Italian Ministry of Finance* Case 33/70 [1970] ECR 1213 judgment, the Court analysed the combined effect of articles 9 and 13(2) of the Treaty regarding the customs union and in particular the abolition of taxes with equivalent effect to customs duties on imports, the decision to accelerate the pace for achieving the customs union and a directive addressed to the Italian State with the purpose of bringing about the date contained in the above decision for the abolition of the tax levied by that State for 'administrative services'.

It found in this connection that: 'Directive No 68/31, the object of which is to impose on a Member State a final date for the performance of a Community obligation, does not concern solely the regulations between the Commission and that State, but also entails legal consequences of which both the other Member States concerned in its performance and individuals may avail themselves when, by its nature, the provision establishing this obligation is directly applicable, as are Articles 9 and 13 of the Treaty, *Sace*.

However, it was not until the *Van Duyn* v *Home Office* Case 41/74 [1974] ECR 1337 judgment that the Court gave a ruling on the direct effect of a provision in a directive taken in isolation. The Court was asked to give a ruling on the right of an individual before a national court to claim the benefit of article 3(1) of the Directive No 64/221 co-ordinating provisions concerning immigration regulations. This article provides that, 'Measures taken on grounds of public policy or of public security shall be based exclusively on the personal conduct of the individual concerned.'

The case concerned a Community national, a member of the Church of Scientology, who had, on this ground, been forbidden access to British territory where she wished to take up employment. The court repeated in full with respect to a directive the findings it had made in the *Grad* judgment. It went on to examine the nature, the subject matter and the terms of the provision in question and concluded that the latter gave rise to rights enforceable at law for the benefit of individuals.

The judgment was followed by several others dealing with the same subject: the direct effect of provisions in Directive No 64/221 on immigration regulations.

Two later judgments must also be mentioned because of the powers they grant to the national courts in ensuring that national implementing measures conform to directives.

The first case concerned the application of the principles of deductibility of the amount of VAT paid on goods acquired for the requirements of a business and the option open to the Member States to derogate from these principles in the case of 'capital goods'.

The plaintiff company had claimed in the national proceedings that the concept of 'capital goods' had been interpreted too widely by the Netherlands. The national court had asked the Court of Justice whether the party had a right to unlimited deduction which the courts must protect. After recalling the classic grounds of judgment in the *Grad* and *Van Duyn* cases and especially the right of interested parties to rely in law on a provision in a directive, the Court added, 'This is especially so when the individual invokes a provision of a directive before a national court in order that the latter shall rule whether the competent national authorities, in exercising the choice which is left to them as to the form and the methods for implementing the directives, have kept within the limits as to their discretion set out in the directive.' *Verbond Van Nederlandse Ondernemingen* v *Inspecteur der Invoerrechten* Case 51/76 [1977] ECR 113.

In the *Enka* case Case 38/77 [1977] ECR 2203 the point at issue was the method of calculating the customs value of goods imported from a 'new' Member state into an 'old' Member State. A directive forbade the costs of warehousing and preserving the goods from being incorporated into the 'price paid or payable' when calculating the customs duty. Could an individual invoke this rule for his own benefit? After referring to its earlier decisions and especially to paragraph 24 of its judgment in the *Verbond Van Nederlandse Ondernemingen* case quoted above, the Court added:

'It emerges from the third paragraph of article 189 of the Treaty that the choice left to the Member States as regards the form of the measures and the methods used in their adoption by the national authorities depends upon the results which the Council or the Commission wishes to see achieved.'

In the case in question, it appears from the Community rules that the intention of the directive is to achieve strict uniformity in the national provisions governing the treatment of imported goods. The Court concluded that: 'As regards the concept of the 'price paid or payable' referred to in article 9 of Regulation No 803/68 the directive leaves the national authorities no area of discretion, with the result that the terms of the directive must prevail over any provisions which may be incompatible with it in each Member State.'

It is clear that the key concept is and remains the existence of discretionary powers with the Member States. Direct effect only exists in so far as there is no such power or a proposition which can be discerned more easily where the directive in question has not been implemented by the State within the period prescribed for its implementation. *Ratti* Case 148/78 [1979] ECR 1629. The recent case of *Marshall* v *Southampton and South-West Area Health Authority* Case 152/84 [1986] 1 CMLR 688 is an example of this. It was held that the State could not defend itself on the grounds of its own failure to implement a directive (No 76/207). The effect of course was that a 'vertical' action ie against the State could be brought by an individual, notwithstanding that an 'arbitrary and unfair distinction' would be created between state employees and private employees.

The case begged the question as to what exactly is the State qua employer for the purposes of such an action? Indeed what is the State and its emanations? In *R* v *London Boroughs Transport Committee* [1990] 1 CMLR 229 it was held that since a local authority exercises governmental power it was an emanation of the State. The width of the interpretation of emanation fell to be considered in the Court of Appeal in the case of *Foster and Others* v *British Gas plc*, 1988, where Donaldson MR held that although the ECJ in *Marshall* had held that the health authority was the 'State' the question was really a matter for the English Courts.

He cited the case of *Tamlin* v *Hannaford* [1950] 1 KB 18 which considered the status of the British Transport Commission and approved its finding that the BTC was 'a public authority and no doubt its purposes are public purposes but it is not a government department ...' he concluded that British Gas (pre-privatisation) was not an emanation of State.

Inevitably this case went on appeal to the House of Lords who tabled an article 177 reference to the ECJ. It was held that provisions of a Directive (if they are capable of being directly effective) may be relied upon against an entity which provides a public service under the control of the State and which has powers in excess of those which result from the normal rules applicable in relations between individuals. The legal form of the entity does not matter. Accordingly article 5(1) of Directive 76/207 could be relied on against British Gas (Judgment July 1990)

International agreements concluded by the Community

In view of its decisions on direct effect, the Court was logically bound to admit that the provisions of international agreements concluded by the Community could be invoked by courts and tribunals as elements of Community law.

It did so in the *Bresciani Italian Finance* Case 87/75 [1976] ECR 129 judgment concerning the scope of an article in Yaounde Conventions I and II referring to a provision in the Treaty, article 13(2), which itself has direct effect.

The Court did not merely point to the existence of the reference. It set the provision in the context of the association agreements to which it belonged. It observed that the provision on customs duties on imports was, for the Community, an obligation unqualified by any reservation, either implicit or explicit. Only the associated States could ask for consultations on the subject to be opened and this imbalance in the benefits, normal in agreements of this kind, did not have the result of robbing the provision of direct effect in the relations between the Member States and individuals.

The Court has also recognised the direct effect of provisions in international agreements similar to those contained in the EEC Treaty which did occur in agreements establishing free trade zones between the Community and non-member States, such as the agreements concluded with European countries which are not candidates for accession.

The Association Agreement between the Community and Portugal has been the subject of two recent cases, the first concerning provisions similar to articles 30-36 in the context of copyright and the second concerning a provision similar to the prohibition on discriminatory internal taxation in article 95 in the context of port wine. In *Polydor* v *Harlequin Record Shops* Case 270/80 [1982] ECR 329 the Court did not decide whether provisions similar to articles 30-36 were of direct effect but held that the interpretation by the Court of articles 30-36 of the EEC Treaty could not be transposed to the EEC/Portugal Agreement since the objectives of the two treaties are different, the latter only being intended to establish a customs union while the former was designed to go further and to unite national markets into a single common market. However, in *Haupzollamt Mainz* v *Kupferberg* Case 104/81 [1983] CMLR 1 the Court held that article 21 of the EEC/Portugal agreement was of direct effect because of the specific object of article 21 in the system of rules laid down by the agreement and its terms and not because of the nature or status of the agreement. But it gave a more restrictive interpretation to article 21 than it has given to article 95 of the EEC Treaty.

On the other hand, in respect of the GATT and the tariff protocols thereto, the Court has very recently held that it has power to interpret these provisions but that they are not of direct effect and do not confer rights on individuals to be enforced by the national courts. (See Joined Cases 267/81, 268/81, and 269/81).

The status of a national rule contrary to a rule with direct effect

In the Court's view, national law contrary to a Community rule with direct effect cannot be applied by the courts, but it is for the legal system in each State to decide the legal procedure by which this result is to be achieved.

The Court stated in the *Luck* v *Hauptzollampt Koln-Rheinau* Case 34/67 [1968] ECR 115 judgment that the national court must not apply a national rule conflicting with a Community provision having direct effect. The same solution was repeated in the *Lorenz* (above) judgment and more recently still, in the *Simmenthal* case Case 92/78 [1979] ECR 777 we read that: 'The relationship between provisions of the Treaty and directly applicable measures of the institutions on the one hand and the national law of the Member States on the other is such that those provisions and measures by their entry into force render automatically inapplicable any conflicting provision of current national law. The recognised right of the domestic order to choose the most appropriate procedure for ensuring the direct effect of Community law must be reconciled with the fact that its provisions are an immediate source of rights and obligations for all concerned.'

Thus, at the very least, national courts must refrain from applying contrary earlier law. The courts will be able to go further and, for example, declare the contrary provisions null and void where the national law affords them such power.

By virtue of the primacy of Community law, the 'blocking effect' of directly applicable provisions is also apparent with regard to subsequent national law. As has been seen, this may occur with provisions implementing a directive. In the *Simmenthal* judgment, the Court strongly emphasised that directly applicable provisions of Community law had the effect of preventing the 'valid adoption of new national legislative measures to the extent to which they would be incompatible with Community provisions'. Such acts being invalid the national courts cannot give effect to them.

The limits of direct effect

Although, to repeat the Court's words once again, 'direct applicability ... means that the rules of Community law must be fully and uniformly applied in all the Member States from the date of their entry into force and for so long as they continue in force', the principle of the States' so-called procedural autonomy may result in differences in the actual application of Community Law.

It is for national courts to ensure that their subjects benefit from the legal protection arising from the direct effect of Community law: see *Rewe-Zentralfinanz* v *Saarland* Case 33/76 [1977] CMLR 533. The national courts must apply the rules of domestic procedural law.

In the *Comet* v *Produktschap Voor Siergewassen* Case 45/76 [1977] 1 CMLR 533 judgment, the Court gave the following ruling on this point: 'In the absence of any relevant Community rules, it is for the national legal order of each Member State to designate the competent courts and to lay down the procedural rules for proceedings designed to ensure the protection of rights which individuals acquire through the direct effect of Community law, provided that such rules are not less favourable than those governing the same right of action on an internal matter. The position would be different only if those rules and time-limits made it impossible in practice to exercise rights which the national courts have a duty to protect.'

This judgment concerns limitation periods fixed by domestic law for actions for the recovery of taxes collected contrary to Community law. On the facts, the Court found that the limitation periods concerned were reasonable.

The principle of legal certainty, applicable to domestic law as to Community law, justified fixing such periods. Where there are no procedural rules under Community law, it is national law which is applicable.

The absence of any co-ordination of domestic procedural rules, necessarily entails the existence of different limitation periods and therefore a certain divergence in the actual application of Community law. It is possible that similar observations might be made with respect to the system of national penalties for infringements of Community law and the procedure for bringing actions. There is no doubt that in these matters there is a wide divergence between the various domestic systems. The obligation to co-operate incumbent on the Member States by virtue of article 5 of the Treaty seems quite inadequate to meet these divergences which are rooted in history. Only co-ordinating actions initiated by the Community or spontaneously by the Member States with a view to the approximation of national laws can, in the long term, reduce these differences. (See in this context, *R* v *Goldstein*.)

6 Primacy of Community Law

General
UK

General

It is in *Costa* v *Ente Nationale per l'Energia Electrica* Case 6/64 [1964] CMLR 425 that the Court established its doctrine of the primacy of Community law.

The facts behind the case are simple: an individual was claiming before his local court - the *guidice conciliatore* of Milan - that the law nationalising production and distribution of electricity was incompatible with the EEC Treaty. The local court referred several questions to the Court of Justice for a preliminary ruling. The Italian Government maintained that the proceedings were totally inadmissible because, in the case in question, the Italian court was only entitled to apply the nationalisation law and not the law approving the Treaty, since the latter law was earlier. This argument was based on a judgment given by the Italian constitutional court in a case between the same parties. The decision had aroused legitimate concern in Community circles.

It is understandable that the Court of Justice decided to take a stand on the problem. In any case, the procedural objection raised, left it no option. The judgment in *Costa* v *ENEL* plays the same role with regard to primacy as the judgment in *Van Gend en Loos* Case 26/62: see Chapter 5 with regard to direct effect. Primacy is the corollary of the Court's conception of the Community legal order as being 'integrated into the legal systems of the Member States and binding on their courts'.

At the outset of the previous chapter those passages from the judgment were cited in which the Court described the legal order resulting from the Treaties.

The Court there emphasised the unlimited duration of the Community, the autonomy of Community power, both internally and externally, and especially the limitation of competence or transfer of powers from the States to the Community. The close connections between direct effect and primacy are clear. These twin pillars of the Community legal order are necessarily implied by the refashioning of powers entailed in the establishment of the Communities.

The Court was determined to show that the 'words and spirit of the Treaty' necessarily implied that, 'it is impossible for the States to set up a subsequent unilateral measure against a legal order which they have accepted on a reciprocal basis'. It is not possible to repeat here the textual arguments which do not perhaps have the same force as those based on the description of the essential characteristics of the Community legal order. It should be pointed out, however, that the Court finds the primacy of Community law confirmed by the wording of article 189 under which regulations have 'binding' force and are 'directly applicable to all Member States'. In so doing, the Court emphasises afresh the connection not only between direct applicability and primacy, but also between the latter and the legislative power conferred on the Community. The Court points out that this provision, which is not qualified by any reservation, 'would be meaningless if a State could unilaterally nullify its effect by means of legislative measures which could prevail over Community law'. Any claim that a State might have to give precedence to a later law over a regulation is moreover rendered absurd simply by the fact that a subsequent regulation could put an end to this inconsistency.

The Court was thus able to reach a conclusion in words which have become classic and have had considerable influence in national decisions:

* 'It follows from all these observations that the law stemming from the * Treaty, an independent source of law, could not, because of its special and original nature, be overridden by domestic legal provisions, however framed, without being deprived of its character as Community law and without the legal basis of the Community itself being called into question. The transfer by the States from their domestic legal system to the Community legal system of rights and obligations arising under the Treaty carries with it a permanent limitation of their sovereign rights against which a subsequent unilateral act incompatible with the concept of the Community cannot prevail.'

It is the Treaty which is the real source of primacy and not the provisions of the national constitutions. There is, accordingly, no need to rely on constitutional rules, either written or unwritten, governing relations between international law and national law. Because of its 'special and original' nature Community law must be accorded primacy.

The Court's ruling is addressed directly to national courts. Its decisions cannot be regarded as an expression of the practical necessity which has always led international courts to assert the superiority of the law they are applying over national law, the latter being sometimes treated as simply a question of fact. This dualism is not appropriate in the relations between the Community legal order and the national orders. It gives a poor idea of the co-ordination between them, which finds expression especially in the machinery for seeking preliminary rulings. Thus when the Court rules that domestic law cannot override Community law, it is referring to proceedings before national courts. This is even clearer in *Simmenthal SpA* v *Commission* Case 92/78 [1979] ECR 777 where the Court concluded that:

'Every national court must, in a case within its jurisdiction, apply Community law in its entirety and protect rights which the latter confers on individuals and must accordingly set aside any provision of national law which may conflict with it, whether prior or subsequent to the Community rule.'

Primacy is not an obligation which it is incumbent upon the founder of the constitution or the legislator to implement. It is a rule to be applied by the Courts.

This rule is therefore unconditional. It is also absolute in the sense that it applies to every rule of domestic law, whatever its standing, even if it is a constitutional rule. Suggested discreetly in the *Costa* judgment as appears in the passage quoted above, the principle of the primacy of Community law over national constitutions has been developed and amplified in later judgments.

In the *San Michel* v *HA of ECSC* Case 9/65 [1967] ECR 1 an undertaking bringing an action for annulment of a decision by the High Authority imposing payment of an equalisation charge on imported ferrous and similar scrap asked the Court of Justice to suspend judgment until the constitutional court had given judgment on the alleged unconstitutionality of certain provisions in the ECSC Treaty. The Court, of course, disallowed this request because 'all States have adhered to the Treaty on the same conditions, definitely and without any reservations, other than those set out in the supplementary protocols, and therefore any claims by a national of a Member State questioning such adherence would be contrary to the system of Community law.'

The Court thus emphasises that any claim by a State to give its own constitutional rules precedence over Community rules is bound to disrupt the Community and is contrary to the principle of accession on a reciprocal basis already mentioned in the *Costa* judgment. The Court is touching here on a fundamental fact of the process of integration. States can only accept the limitations of sovereignty corresponding to important changes of power if the rules to which they submit are genuinely common. This is not the case if the rules are subject to criteria and procedures which necessarily differ from one State to another.

The Court has recalled these principles several times.

In *Internationale Handelsgesellschaft GmbH* v *Einfuhr und Vorratsstelle fur Getreide und Futtermittel* Case 11/70 [1970] ECR 1125 the judgment repeated word for word one of the grounds of judgment in the *Costa* v *ENEL* case and added that:

'The validity of a Community measure or its effect within a Member State cannot be affected by allegations that it runs counter to either fundamental rights as formulated by the constitution of the State or the principles of a national constitutional structure.'

In the *Leonesio* v *Italian Ministry of Agriculture* Case 93/71 [1972] ECR 287 judgment referred to above, the Court disallowed the claim of a State which wished to make the payment of a premium for the slaughter of cows under Community provisions dependent on the adoption of budgetary provisions, although all the necessary conditions had been satisfied by the claimant.

A little later, with regard to the same State, the Court held, this time in connection with premiums for grubbing fruit trees, that:

'A Member State cannot plead the provisions or practices of its internal order in order to justify failure to observe obligations and time limits arising from Community regulations; it falls to a Member State, in accordance with the general obligations imposed on Member States by article 4 of the Treaty, to recognise the consquences in its internal order to its adherence to the Community and, if necessary, to adapt its procedures for budgetary provision in such a way that they do not form an obstacle to the implementations, within the prescribed time-limits, of its obligations within the framework of the Treaty.'.

See also *Amsterdam Bulb BV* v *Produktschap Voor Siergewassen* Case 50/76 [1977] 2 CMLR 218 and *Commission* v *Council (ERTA)* Case 22/70 [1971] CMLR 335 where community law was held to be supreme not only over domestic law but also over a Member State's obligations to other states.

UK

In the UK, the European Communities Act 1972 makes all Community law provisions, which are directly effective, part of national law s2(1). Further s2(4) states that 'any enactment passed or to be passed, other than one contained in this Part of this Act, shall be construed and have effect subject to the foregoing provisions of this section.' This has been held by some to mean that the national courts must interpret Community law 'in accordance with the principles laid down by and any relevant decision of the European Court' s3(1) and so acknowledge the supremacy of Community law. It has been further contended that the foregoing places duty on the national courts to interpret national laws so as to give effect to provisions of Community law. This proposition relies on the judgment in Case 14/83 *Von Colson* [1984] ECR 1891 part of which states that national courts are required to interpret this national law (legislation introduced to implement Directive 76/297) in the light of the wording and purpose of the directive.

In *Duke* v *GEC Reliance* [1988] 1 All ER 626 the House of Lords grappled with this thorny issue. The facts involved the issue of whether an individual who could not rely on an unimplemented directive, (76/207), as it was only vertically directly effective, could rely on a section in a statute (s6 Sex Discrimination Act 1975) coupled with the argument that the statute had to be interpreted in such a way as to give effect to the directive.

Lord Templeman stated that in his view s2(4) European Communities Act 1972 does not allow or 'constrain a British court to distort the meaning of a British statute in order to enforce against an individual a Community directive which has no direct effect between individuals.' Lord Templeman preferred the part of the *Von Colson* judgment which stated that 'it is for the national court to interpret and apply the legislation adopted for the implementation of the directive in conformity with requirements of Community law.' The Sex Discrimination Act 1975 preceded the Directive so was clearly not an Act adopted for the implementation of the directive in question. The House of Lords stated that s2(4) ECA 1972 only required the national courts to construe Acts of Parliament in accordance with directly effective provisions of Community law and in the present case the directive was clearly not directly effective. This case did not advance knowledge of the issue of primacy in the English courts but the later case No C-213/89 *R* v *Secretary of State for Transport ex parte Factortame Ltd and Others* (19 June 1990) sheds important new light on the conflict between Community law and the national law and leaves no doubt what the duty of the national courts is to be. The arguments in the case concerned, inter alia, the question of whether the UK courts had powers to suspend the operation of a statute or order an injunction against the Government pending a ruling from the ECJ. The ECJ determined where a reference + has been made to the ECJ an English court may suspend the operation of an Act of Parliament or grant an injunction against the Government even if, under national law, it has no power to do so.

+ UK court may suspend the operation of a Statute or order an injunction against the govt. pending a ruling from the ECJ. – even if under UK law it has no power to do so.

Index

HOLBORN COLLEGE COURSES

SPECIALIST DIPLOMAS IN LAW & BUSINESS

Validated by the University of Oxford Delegacy of Local Examinations at degree level.

9 month course.

Diplomas in: Contract Law • Commercial Law • Company Law • Revenue Law • European Community Law • Criminal Law • Evidence • Constitutional Law • English Legal System • Land Law • Organisational Theory • Economics • Accounting and Business Finance • Computer Systems & Information Technology • Maths for Economists • Statistics

Entry: Evidence of sufficient academic or work experience to study at degree level.

FUNDAMENTALS OF BRITISH BUSINESS

Examined internally by Holborn College

To familiarise European and other overseas business studies students with UK business practice. Courses are tailor-made for groups of students on a College to College basis. Courses run for ten to seventeen weeks and permit part-time relevant work experience.

Past courses have included: Aspects of Organisational Behaviour • Marketing • Statistics • Business English & Communication Skills • Economics • International Trade • Company Law

LAW

Examined externally by the University of London.

Three year course.

LLB Law.

Entry: 2 'A' levels grade E and 3 'O' levels.

ACCOUNTING & MANAGEMENT DEGREES

Examined externally by the University of London.

Three year course.

BSc (Econ) Accounting • BSc (Econ) Management Studies • BSc (Econ) Economics & Management Studies

Entry: 2 'A' levels grade E and 3 'O' levels to include Maths and English.

DIPLOMA IN ECONOMICS.

Examined externally by the University of London.

One year full time, two year part time courses.

Completion of the Diploma gives exemption from the first year of the BSc (Econ) Degree programmes reducing them to two years.

Entry: Mathematics and English 'O' level equivalent. Minimum age 18.

THE COMMON PROFESSIONAL EXAMINATION

Examined externally by Wolverhampton Polytechnic.

9 month, 6 month and short revision courses.

Entry: Acceptance by the Professional Body.

THE BAR EXAMINATION

Examined by the Council of Legal Education for non-UK practitioners.

9 month course.

Entry: Acceptance by the Professional Body.

THE SOLICITORS' FINAL

Examined by the Law Society.

6 month re-sit and short revision courses.

Entry: Acceptance by the Professional Body.

THE INSTITUTE OF LEGAL EXECUTIVES FINAL PART 2

Examined by the Institute of Legal Executives.

9 month course and short revision courses.

Entry: Acceptance by the Professional Body.

A & AS LEVEL COURSES

Examined by various UK Boards.

9 month course and short revision courses

Subjects offered: Law • Constitutional Law • Economics • Accounting • Business Studies • Mathematics Pure and Applied • Mathematics and Statistics • Sociology • Government and Politics

Entry: 3 'O' levels.

FULL-TIME, PART-TIME, REVISION & DISTANCE LEARNING

cut along dotted line

ORDER FORM

LLB PUBLICATIONS	TEXTBOOKS Cost £	£	CASEBOOKS Cost £	£	REVISION WORKBOOKS Cost £	£	SUG. SOL. 1985/89 Cost £	£	SUG. SOL. 1990 Cost £	£
Administrative Law	17.95		18.95				14.95		3.00	
Commercial Law Vol I	17.95		18.95		9.95		14.95		3.00	
Vol II	16.95		18.95							
Company Law	18.95		18.95		9.95		14.95		3.00	
Conflict of Laws	17.95		16.95							
Constitutional Law	13.95		16.95		9.95		14.95		3.00	
Contract Law	13.95		16.95		9.95		14.95		3.00	
Conveyancing	16.95		16.95							
Criminal Law	13.95		16.95		9.95		14.95		3.00	
Criminology	16.95									
European Community Law	17.95		16.95						3.00	
English Legal System	13.95		14.95				*7.95		3.00	
Equity and Trusts	13.95		18.95		9.95		14.95		3.00	
Evidence	17.95		17.95		9.95		14.95		3.00	
Family Law	16.95		18.95		9.95		14.95		3.00	
Jurisprudence	14.95				9.95		14.95		3.00	
Labour Law	15.95									
Land Law	13.95		18.95		9.95		14.95		3.00	
Public International Law	18.95		16.95		9.95		14.95		3.00	
Revenue Law	16.95		18.95		9.95		14.95		3.00	
Roman Law	19.95									
Succession	16.95		17.95		9.95		14.95		3.00	
Tort	13.95		18.95		9.95		14.95		3.00	
CPE PUBLICATIONS										
Criminal Law	13.95									
Constitutional & Administrative Law	13.95									
Contract Law	13.95									
Equity and Trusts	13.95									
Land Law	13.95									
Tort	13.95									
BAR PUBLICATIONS										
Conflict of Laws	16.95		17.95				† 3.95		3.95	
European Community Law & Human Rights	17.95		16.95				† 3.95		3.95	
Evidence	17.95		17.95				14.95		3.95	
Family Law	16.95		18.95				14.95		3.95	
General Paper I	19.95		16.95				14.95		3.95	
General Paper II	19.95		16.95				14.95		3.95	
Law of International Trade	16.95		16.95				14.95		3.95	
Practical Conveyancing	16.95		16.95				14.95		3.95	
Procedure	19.95		16.95				14.95		3.95	
Revenue Law	16.95		18.95				14.95		3.95	
Sale of Goods and Credit	17.95		17.95				14.95		3.95	

* 1987-1989 papers only † 1988 and 1989 papers only

SOLICITORS' FINAL	TEXTBOOKS		REVISION WORKBOOKS		SUGGESTED SOLUTIONS							
					PACKS (a)				SINGLE PAPERS (b)			
					Winter		Summer		Winter		Summer	
	Cost £	£	Cost £	£	Cost £	£	Cost £	£	Cost £	£	Cost £	£
Accounts	14.95		9.95		14.95		14.95		2.25		2.25	
Business Organisations &Insolvency	14.95				11.95		§ 11.95		2.25		2.25	
Consumer Protection & Employment Law	14.95				11.95		§ 11.95		2.25		2.25	
Conveyancing I & II	14.95				14.95		14.95		2.25		2.25	
Family Law	14.95				14.95		14.95		2.25		2.25	
Litigation	14.95				14.95		14.95		2.25		2.25	
Wills, Probate & Administration	14.95		9.95		14.95		14.95		2.25		2.25	
Final Exam Papers (Set) (All Papers) 1989							9.95					
Final Exam Papers (Set) (All Papers) 1990					9.95		9.95					
INSTITUTE OF LEGAL EXECUTIVES												
Company & Partnership Law	18.95											
Constitutional Law	13.95											
Contract Law	13.95											
Criminal Law	13.95											
Equity and Trusts	13.95											
European Law & Practice	17.95											
Evidence	17.95											
Land Law	13.95											
Revenue Law	16.95											
Tort	13.95											

§ Limited to new syllabus from Summer 1986.

(a) Packs consist of either collected Winter or Summer papers. They change in April to include the previous Summer & Winter papers respectively.

(b) Single papers are published in April & October and are the previous Winter & Summer papers respectively, together with final examination papers.

HLT PUBLICATIONS

All HLT Publications have two important qualities. First, they are written by specialists, all of whom have direct practical experience of teaching the syllabus. Second, all Textbooks are reviewed and updated each year to reflect new developments and changing trends.

They are used widely by students at polytechnics and colleges throughout the United Kingdom and overseas.

A comprehensive range of titles is covered by the following classifications.

- **TEXTBOOKS**
- **CASEBOOKS**
- **SUGGESTED SOLUTIONS**
- **REVISION WORKBOOKS**

The books listed overleaf can be ordered through your local bookshops or obtained direct from the publisher using this order form. Telephone, Fax, or Telex orders will also be accepted. Quote your Access or Visa card numbers for priority orders. To order direct from publisher please enter cost of titles you require, fill in despatch details and send it with your remittance to The HLT Group Ltd.

Please complete Order Form overleaf

DETAILS FOR DESPATCH OF PUBLICATIONS

Please insert your full name below

Please insert below the style in which you would like the correspondence from the Publisher addressed to you

TITLE Mr, Miss etc. INITIALS SURNAME/FAMILY NAME

Address to which study material is to be sent (please ensure someone will be present to accept delivery of your Publications).

POSTAGE & PACKING

You are welcome to purchase study material from the Publisher at 200 Greyhound Road, London W14 9RY, during normal working hours.

If you wish to order by post this may be done direct from the Publisher. Postal charges are as follows:

UK - Orders over £30: no charge. Orders below £30: £2.00. Single paper (last exam only): 40p

OVERSEAS - See table below

The Publisher cannot accept responsibility in respect of postal delays or losses in the postal systems.

DESPATCH All cheques must be cleared before material is despatched.

SUMMARY OF ORDER

Date of order:

£

Cost of publications ordered:

Add postage and packing: UNITED KINGDOM:

OVERSEAS:	TEXTS		Suggested Solutions (last Exam only)
	One	Each Extra	
Eire	£3.00	£0.50	£1.00
European Community	£7.50	£0.50	£1.00
East Europe & North America	£8.50	£1.00	£1.50
South East Asia	£10.00	£1.50	£1.50
Australia / New Zealand	£12.00	£3.50	£1.50
Other Countries (Africa, India etc)	£11.00	£3.00	£1.50

Total cost of order: £

Please ensure that you enclose a cheque or draft payable to The HLT Group Ltd for the above amount, or charge to ☐ Access ☐ Visa

Card Number

Expiry Date ____________ Signature ____________